C000172880

STUART MCHARDY has lectured and wr̲ history and folklore both in Scotland a̲ all aspects of Scottish culture led to his president of the Pictish Arts Society. Director of the Scots Language Reso                        ...... Following many years on the seminal 'McGregor's Gathering' (BBC Radio Scotland) he has continued to broadcast on radio and television. He lectures annually at Edinburgh University's Centre for Continuing Education in the areas of Scottish mythology, folklore and legend. He is also the author of a children's book, *The Wild Haggis and the Greetin-faced Nyaff* (Scottish Children's Press, 1995) and has had poetry in Scots and English published in many magazines. Born in Dundee, McHardy is a graduate of Edinburgh University and lives in that city today with his wife Sandra and their son Roderick.

# Scotland:
# Myth, Legend & Folklore

STUART McHARDY

**Luath** Press Limited
EDINBURGH
www.luath.co.uk

First Published 1999

The paper used in this book is acid-free, neutral-sized and recyclable.
It is made from low chlorine pulps produced in a low energy,
low emission manner from sustainable forests.

Printed and bound by
Bell & Bain Ltd., Glasgow

Maps by Jim Lewis

Illustrations by Nulsh the Bold, Scottish Cartoon Art Studio, Glasgow

Edited by Varese Layzer

Typeset in 10.5 point Sabon by
S. Fairgrieve, Edinburgh 0131 658 1763

© Stuart McHardy

In Memoriam

Martin Hendry

1943-1999

# Contents

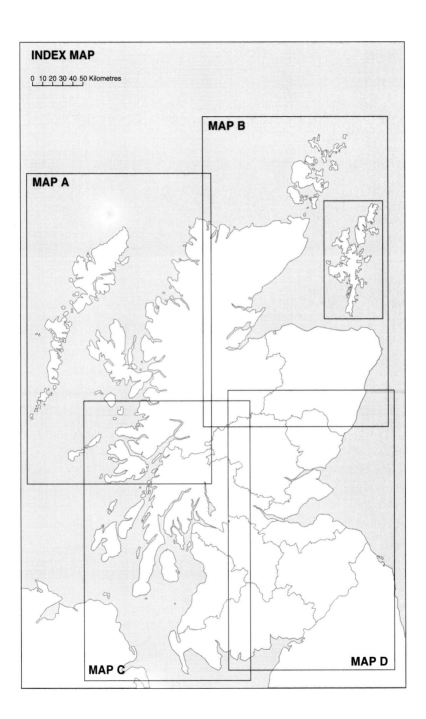

**INDEX MAP**

0 10 20 30 40 50 Kilometres

MAP B

MAP A

MAP C

MAP D

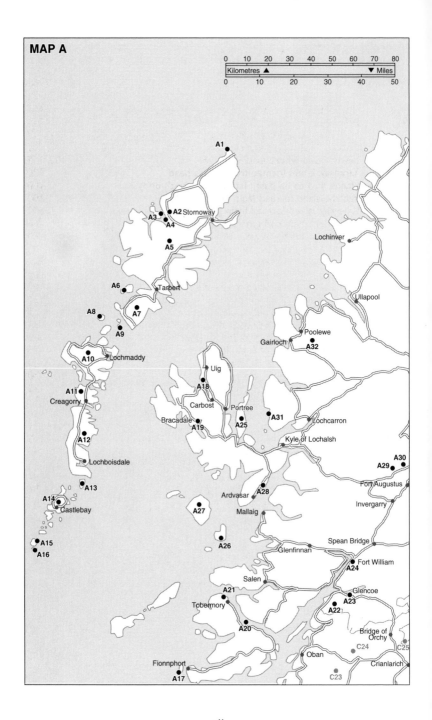

# MAP A

0  10  20  30  40  50  60  70  80
Kilometres ▲          ▼ Miles
0  10  20  30  40  50

A1

A2 Stornoway
A3
A4

Lochinver

A5

A6    Tarbert

Ullapool

A8        A7

A9                          Gairloch    Poolewe
                                        A32
A10   Lochmaddy

A11                        Uig
Creagorry              A18
                    Carbost    Portree
A12            Bracadale      A25    A31    Lochcarron
                        A19
         Lochboisdale                Kyle of Lochalsh

A13                                              A30
A14                                        A29
Castlebay                              Fort Augustus
                    Ardvasar   A28
A15            A27         Mallaig      Invergarry
A16
                                  Spean Bridge
                A26        Glenfinnan
                                        Fort William
                    Salen            A24
                A21                      Glencoe
         Tobermory              A23
                              A22
                A20                  Bridge of
                                     Orchy
                                          C24      C25
Fionnphort                    Oban
                                          Crianlarich
A17                              C23

xii

# Key to Map A

xiv

# Key to Map B

# Key to Map C

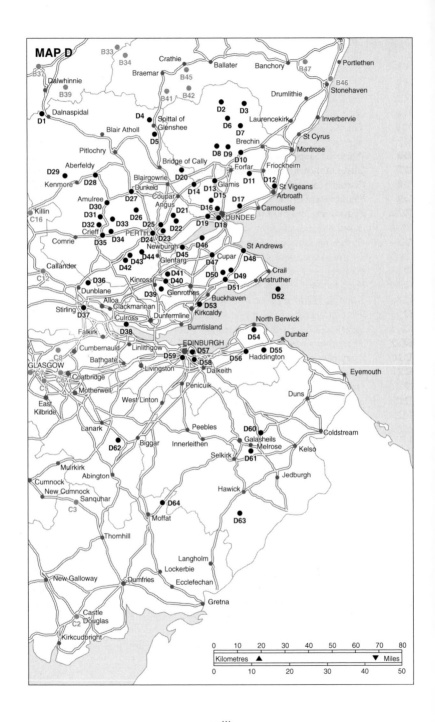

MAP D

B33  B34  Crathie  Ballater  Banchory  B47  Portlethen
B37
B39  Dalwhinnie  Braemar  B45  Drumlithie  B46  Stonehaven
Dalnaspidal  B41  B42  Inverbervie
D1  Blair Atholl  D2  D3  Laurencekirk  St Cyrus
Pitlochry  Spittal of  D6  D7  Brechin  Montrose
D4  Glenshee  D8  D9  Forfar  Friockheim
Aberfeldy  D5  Bridge of Cally  D10  D11  D12  St Vigeans
D29  Blairgowrie  Glamis  Arbroath
Kenmore  D28  Dunkeld  D20  D14  D13  D17  Carnoustie
Amulree  Coupar  D15
Killin  D30  D27  Angus  D16  DUNDEE
C16  D31  D26  D21
D32  D33  D25  D22  D19  D18
Crieff  D35  D34  D24  D23  D46  St Andrews
Comrie  PERTH  Newburgh  D45  Cupar  D48
Callander  D36  Glenfarg  D47  D49  Crail
C12  D43  D44  D41  D50  Anstruther
Dunblane  Kinross  D40  D51  D52
D42  Glenrothes  Buckhaven
Alloa  D39  D53
Stirling  Clackmannan  Kirkcaldy
D37  Culross  Dunfermline  North Berwick
Falkirk  Burntisland  D54  Dunbar
D38  Linlithgow  EDINBURGH  D55
Cumbernauld  D59  D57  D56  Haddington
C8  Bathgate  D58  Dalkeith  Eyemouth
GLASGOW  Livingston  Penicuik
C6  Coatbridge  Duns
C5  Motherwell
East  West Linton  Coldstream
Kilbride  Peebles  D60
Lanark  Innerleithen  Galasheils  Kelso
Biggar  Melrose
D62  Selkirk  D61
Muirkirk  Jedburgh
Cumnock  Abington  Hawick
New Cumnock  Sanquhar  D64
C3  D63
Thornhill  Moffat
Langholm
New Galloway  Lockerbie
Ecclefechan
Dumfries
Castle  Gretna
Douglas
Kirkcudbright

0  10  20  30  40  50  60  70  80
Kilometres  ▲  ▼  Miles
0  10  20  30  40  50

xviii

# Key to Map D

# Preface

AS A CHILD TOURING SCOTLAND I constantly nagged my parents to visit stone circles, brochs and standing stones. As I grew older I began to realise that many of these ancient sites had stories told of them and I found these stories as entrancing as the sites themselves. These stories were originally handed down through the generations by word of mouth, in Gaelic, Norse or Scots. They survived because they had meaning for both the people telling them and the people listening to them. Before writing this was how all human knowledge was transmitted; tales and legends were of central importance to human society. If they had no significance they would not have survived long enough to have been written down. For many years I have been researching Scottish legend and folklore and though there is much in common with the lore of other countries like England, Ireland, Scandinavia and Wales, our culture is uniquely our own.

I have spent much of my life researching Scotland's past to try and gain a clearer understanding of who I am. What I have found is that Scotland is not a Celtic country but a Scottish country in which traditions and beliefs often called 'Celtic' are just as rooted in the traditions of Germanic-speaking peoples, like the Scandinavians, the English, and of course Scots speakers. The old phrase 'We're aw Jock Tamson's bairns' perhaps deserves a postscript: we're aw mongrels as weel. The traditions and tales in this book are intended to illustrate the diversity and complexity of Scottish culture.

Scotland's landscape is renowned for its beauty and visitors flock here from all over the world despite our often atrocious weather. I hope these stories show that our landscape is not just rich in beauty but also rich in lore and legend created over thousands of years. As we enter a new and potentially exciting political situation it is important that we try and get as clear a picture as we can of who we are and where we come from.

*Stuart McHardy*

# Introduction

People come from all over the world to visit Scotland. Its beauty is well known – the magnificent mountains, the lonely glens and lush straths, tumbling rivers and placid lochs – all can touch the heart and stir the soul.

For all the vastness of the Scottish landscape, each of its mountains has a particular story connected to it. From the dawn of time, the myths and legends of Scotland and the exploits of those who lived here have come down to us in stories in Gaelic and Scots, tales from times when those languages themselves had yet to breathe.

Writing came to Europe only a few thousand years ago and much of the material in this book comes from before then. People then loved their land even more than we do today: they saw themselves as tied to it in ways modern city-dwellers have long forgotten. Much of the material in this book comes directly from those ancient times, reworkings of the great themes of life and death, love and liberty, told against the background of the Scottish landscape. It was and is a landscape of the eye, the heart and the soul of the peoples who have lived here. Magical animals, supernatural beings, heroes, giants and goddesses walk this landscape. As the ancient art of storytelling bursts into new flower, many of these tales are being told again as they once were.

Many things have changed over the past centuries – languages, religions, technology – but the love of the land survives, the glory in its splendour which informs the substance of its legends. What they tell us above all is that we are not so different from our far-off ancestors, and perhaps in the face of environmental destruction and world-wide pollution we may yet learn from them how to live in better harmony with the earth.

The past few decades have seen a world-wide resurgence of people wanting to know more about their 'roots', especially in Europe. Although there are varying reactions all over the world to this situation, here in Scotland we have our own way of doing things. There is a growing interest and participation in the rituals surrounding such ancient sites as the Clootie Well (B13) on the Black Isle, north of Inverness. This ancient sacred well is now a well-known tourist spot and people come from great distances to tie a rag to the trees adjoining the well and to make their wish. This is simply the continuation of an old tradition, once extremely widespread. In this book we shall look at some of the sites and rituals associated with this kind of ancient well-worship.

But there are examples of rituals practised even in Scotland's cities today. Calton Hill (D57) in Edinburgh – itself a name redolent of ancient belief – is the traditional site for a Beltane fire ceremony which has just been revived. It is now attended by thousands as dusk falls on the 31 April (following the traditional way of counting the new day from when the old one dies). This fire festival once took place all over Britain, a rite of sanctity and fertility. Though the actual ceremony today owes more to Mediterranean influences than traditional Scottish behaviour, the celebration and the use of fire, ritual dance and music all echo the May Day rites that seem to have come from the dawn of time. Other parts of Scotland too have seen their own Beltane fires lit, and other fire festivals such as the Burnin o the Clavie at Burghead (B21) or the Up-Hellya Festival in Shetland are immensely popular.

People are drawn to other ancient sites such as stone circles and these have been the focus of many different types of activity. Some people see happenings, like the reborn druids with their midsummer ceremonies at Stonehenge, as central in new forms of pagan worship. Yet others think they may attract UFOs, since suggestions have been made that they are some kind of portal between worlds. The fascination of such sites seems to be growing stronger. The continuing attraction of Arthurian material has been matched over the past few years by a distinctly mystical interest in the thoughts and beliefs of our Celtic ancestors. More books than ever are published on Celtic and even Pictish subjects but we must remember not to lose our critical faculties. The term Celtic, which should apply only to linguistic matters, now surfaces in all sorts of areas and I suppose it is only a matter of time before Arbroath smokies and Forfar bridies are presented as Celtic food!

4

It has been overlooked by many scholars who have written on 'Celtic' society that the last Celtic-speaking tribal warrior society did not disappear until the eighteenth century in Scotland. When the Highland, Lowland and English followers of Prince Charles Edward Stewart were slaughtered at Culloden on 16 June 1746 it truly was the end o an auld sang. The tribal society of the Gaelic-speaking areas of Scotland was already in terminal decline but it is still a remarkable fact that so little has been written about that society. It is as if the body politic of the British State was put into shock by the Jacobite Rebellion and that Scottish history has been suffering ever since. The classic texts on the Celts concentrate on Irish and Welsh material despite the fact that Celtic society continued for hundreds of years later – here in Scotland. And it was a life in which learning was passed on through story and song.

The history of Scotland has long been obscured because of a few historical events. Little written material survives from ancient times due to various raids and invasions. The earliest of these started in the ninth century with the Vikings, who often raided monasteries – the natural home for written material as well as the precious metals they were seeking. Later came the invasion of the English king Edward Longshanks in the thirteenth century. Edward destroyed all documents he could find as they were sure to undermine his opportunistic and dishonest claims to be sovereign lord of Scotland. What he did not destroy was taken south to England and disappeared.

Later, the Reformation saw the unleashing of fanatical mobs who burned books and destroyed great art, claiming it was all 'Papist'. Because of this and because of the close links between Ireland and Scotland, Scottish culture has come to be presented as an Irish import through Gaelic, or an English import through the medium of Anglo-Saxon, which influenced Scots north of the border.

The heroes that populate our landscape come from various traditions – from the Gaelic Finn Mac Cuill and his Fenian warriors to stories of Arthur and his cheating queen, which have survived from times when people in the Southwest, the East and North spoke an ancestor of modern-day Welsh. There are also tales of giants and giantesses which step straight out of the traditions of

Scandinavia, first told in a language related to the Scots and English we hear today.

Scotland has a complex history indeed and most of it was initially passed on through the spoken word. It is the spoken word attached to the landscape that has provided the material for this book. I have found these stories in earlier published material mainly – often guidebooks and local histories whose authors had no particular interest in legendary material, seeing it only as adding a bit of colour. The nineteenth century in particular saw many such publications, triggered by the start of tourism, given such powerful impetus by the works of Sir Walter Scott. Today as we begin to realise we have had little access to Scotland's actual history, such material takes on new significance.

Recent research in Australia has shown the capability of oral tradition to pass on factual material over thousands of years. Aboriginal tales of giant marsupials, for example, had been dismissed as the fantasy of primitive savages. Excavation of the bones of such creatures, now called diprodotons, and sometimes found in sites over 20,000 years old, tells a different story. Other tales mention vocanic eruptions that have also since been confirmed by excavation. The fact is that while mainstream European scholarship has long asserted that oral tradiiton was made redundant when writing was introduced, the spoken word has never ceased to be important.

Much of the material in this book has a long pedigree. How long may be impossible to say, but the intriguing possibility is that the story of the raising of the great stone circle of Calanais on Lewis, passed by word of mouth from generation to generation, is true.

Some stories, like those of Finn Mac Cuill or Arthur, exist in many places because they were told in those places and it is part of the traditional art of storytelling to place stories in a landscape the audience knows. Without such location the stories would lose much of their relevance. Such stories include ones of an ancient mother goddess known as the Cailleach in Gaelic and the Carlin in Scots, stories associated with our magnificent and decidedly moody mountains, tales of lochs and rivers inhabited by supernatural creatures, stories of romance and heroism associated with the Picitish symbol stones, tales of revenge and harrowing tales of the persecution of women as witches perhaps because they held on too strongly to the old ways.

We should remember that Scotland has gone through many significant changes since people started arriving here almost 10,000 years ago. Some of these changes we know about, many we never will. What is significant is that the legendary landscape has retained many ancient ideas despite these often substantial changes. The old idea that major change was a result of invasions by increasingly superior and technologically advanced warrior aristocrats is a fantasy of the ruling classes. We now know that the development of new styles of pottery represent technological advance in itself rather than invasion. Language change was also presented as a result of military conquest. The reality is that Scotland has spoken different languages at different times. It has been predominantly P-Celtic-speaking (the ancestor of modern-day Welsh) as well as Q-Celtic-speaking (the ancestor of modern-day Gaelic) and Germanic-speaking, as today, when most of us have Scots or Scottish-English as our first language. However at different times from the eighth to the eleventh centuries there were Germanic-speaking Norse settlements in different parts of the country and there are suggestions today that Germanic speakers settled here during or after the short visitations of the Romans. There are also suggestions that perhaps Germanic tribes were settling our southeastern coasts almost as early as the Gaels are said to have founded Dalriada, around 500 AD.

Legendary material, however, has a way of passing by such upheavals – as if the psycho-sociological relevance of the stories runs deeper than language itself within society. This might explain why we have the Cailleach in Gaelic matched so precisely by the Carlin in Scots.

Maybe the old ways are not yet totally gone. Apart from resurgences of well-dressing and the Beltane fires, and the survivals of other rituals like the various midwinter fire festivals, these tales can perhaps help us see more clearly how our ancestors lived and what they believed. Industrialisation and literacy are, like the habit of living in cities, very recent in terms of the history of this land, and our much-loved landscape retains a great deal from earlier times.

I have divided the book into topics which link tales of similar kinds and hope this will lead the reader into a deeper understanding of our landscape and hopefully also into physical exploration of this beautiful, ever-changing and lore-laden land.

*Stuart McHardy*
Edinburgh, October 1999

CHAPTER I

# The Hollow Hills

IN VARIOUS PARTS OF THE country different heroes are believed to
be resting below ground awaiting the call to come forth to the aid
of Scotland. It may be that such stories are connected to the
ancient beliefs associated with the great chambered cairn burials
known throughout our landscape. Scholars nowadays see these as
communal burials and no longer as the tombs of kings or other
supposed high-status leaders of contemporary society. These
chambered tombs often contained the bones of several individuals,
though not all of the bones. Skulls and thigh bones seemed to
dominate, suggesting a link with the well-known motif on Scottish
gravestones, the skull-and-crossbones, portrayed in countless
Hollywood films as the flag of pirates. It is now thought that these
were the sites of specific rites on the great feast days of the year.
Samhain, today conflated with Halloween, was very much a feast
of the dead in tribal times. The bones were brought forth at these
times and used in rituals in which the spirits of the dead would be
asked to ensure that the seeds planted in the earth would grow in
the coming spring. This also might help to explain the importance
of genealogies or family histories in Scotland, for if you are asking
your ancestors for direct help it seems a good idea to be sure of
who you are talking to! Such genealogies, passed on by word of
mouth, went back for many generations and the seannachie, the
traditional genealogist of the Highland clans, had his counterpart
at the coronation of kings, as well as at the investiture of clan
chiefs.

## The Eildon Hills

The Eildon Hills (D61) to the south of Melrose in the Borders were
known long ago to the invading Romans as Trimontium, the

9

three-peaked hills. It has long been told locally that King Arthur himself is sleeping inside the Eildons awaiting his call to arms.

A local horse-dealer called Canonbie Dick, a fearless character 'wha wid hae sellt a cuddy tae the Deil himsel', was riding home one evening by the Eildons when he was hailed by a man in very old-fashioned dress. He asked to buy the horses Dick had with him and, after some hard bargaining, paid for them in ancient gold coins before disappearing into the night. This happened several times and at last Dick's curiosity got the better of him and he suggested the mysterious stranger take him home for a drink to seal the bargain. Reluctantly, the stranger agreed but warned Dick that he would be going into danger, particularly if he lost his nerve. This only served to intrigue the horse-dealer even more and he urged the stranger to hurry. The stranger led Dick to a hummock on the side of the Eildons still known today as the Lucken Hare, where to Dick's surprise he opened a concealed door in the side of the hill. At once he found himself inside a huge torch-lit cavern full of rows of stalls, and in each stall a sleeping horse waited with a warrior clad in armour. The horses were all black as coal, as was the armour of the sleeping warriors. On a great table lay a massive sword and a horn of like size. The stranger told Dick that he was Thomas of Ercildoun, the famous Thomas the Rhymer, and he uttered the fateful words, 'He that shall sound that horn and draw that sword shall, if his heart fail him not, be king over all broad Britain. But all depends on courage, and much on your taking the sword or horn first.'

Dick took up the horn and with a trembling hand managed to blow a feeble note. In response a thundering sound erupted and the men and horses began to rise. Horses stamped their hooves and snorted as warriors sprang to their feet sword in hand. Dick was terrified and dropped the horn, reaching his hand to lift the enchanted sword. A great voice rang out:

Woe to the coward that ever he was born
Who did not draw the sword before he blew the horn.

At that a mighty wind came up and Dick was tossed in the air and thrown clean out of the cave. He had made the wrong choice. The following morning he was found lying on the hillside by local shepherds. Lifting his head he told his strange story, fell back and died.

A variant on this story is that once the Rhymer has bought enough coal-black horses the warriors will sally forth from their slumbers to put the world to rights. In other legends the sleeping warriors are King Arthur and his knights awaiting the call to come to the aid of Britain.

It is said that the Eildons are where Thomas Learmont of Ercildoun, now called Earlston (D60), was spirited away by the Queen of the Fairies for seven years. When at last he returned he had the gift of prophecy. Thomas of Ercildoun is believed to have been a real figure who lived in the thirteenth century and many folk rhymes and prophecies are attributed to him. The spot where he was spirited away is marked by a stone where there once was an ancient tree – probably a yew – now known as the Eildon Tree Stone. Such is Thomas the Rhymer's hold on imagination that he is mentioned in several of Scotland's earliest histories and is said to have lived in many parts of the country.

Thomas

There are many versions of his story but all agree he was on Eildon when he saw a fair lady dressed all in green, her horse's mane dressed with silver bells, riding towards him. Taken by both her beauty and her majesty, he doffs his hat and kneels before her. She knows who Thomas is and says that she has come to see him. She takes him up behind her on her horse and she heads for Elfinland. When they come to a red river, Thomas asks what river this can be.

'This,' she tells him, 'is the river of blood that is shed on the earth in one day.'

They ride on and come to a crystal river. Again Thomas asks

what river this can be and the Elfin Queen tells him, 'This is the river of tears that is spilled on the earth in one day.'

On and on they ride until they come to a thorny road and Thomas asks what road this can be.

'This is the road you must never set foot on, for this is the road to Hell.'

They ride on and on and come to a great orchard and Thomas asks to be let down so he can have an apple or two for he is hungry and the apples look very fine to him. The Queen tells him he cannot touch them for they are the apples that are made of the curses that fall on the earth in one day. They ride on and she reaches high up into one particular tree and plucks him an apple. She gives him the apple, saying, 'It will give to you a tongue that will never lie.'

And this is how he got the gift of prophecy. They ride further on and at last come to a great and beautiful valley which she tells him is Elfinland. Thomas lived here for seven long years, after which he returned to earth and became a great prophet. It is said that among other things he foretold that the North Sea and the Atlantic Ocean would one day meet through Scotland, and this is taken to mean the Caledonian Canal. Many and varied are the prophecies and rhymes from all over Scotland attributed to Thomas after his return from Elfinland, but a few years later the following is said to have occurred.

A white hind and hart came forth from the forest to Thomas's village. The local people were amazed to see these wondrous creatures in their village and somebody ran to fetch Thomas so he would tell them what this might mean. When Thomas came, he knew at once, bade farewell to his friends and accompanied the deer back into the forest. He was never seen again.

The motif of the deer and particularly the white deer has been associated with pagan religion, and particularly the mother goddess, for thousands of years all over Europe. They were fitting messengers from the Elfin Queen to summon Thomas back to Elfinland.

# *Tomnahurich*

Tomnahurich (B16), the hill of the yew trees, is in the centre of Inverness. In the middle of the last century it was chosen as a cemetery – but the yew tree has long been associated with burial grounds, possibly because it lives so long that it seemed eternal to our ancestors. Some yew trees, like the famous one at Fortingall (D29) in Perthshire, live for thousands of years. The Fortingall yew tree may be the oldest living organism in Europe.

There is story concerning Tomnahurich which has changed its clothes many times over the years.

Not long ago two sturdy but wild-looking, young, kilted lads were seen in the centre of Inverness. Both were carrying bag-pipes and shouting at all the passing cars – in Gaelic. It was just a matter of time before the police were called and the two young lads locked up in the local jail. In the morning they appeared before the sheriff, who fortunately had the Gaelic himself. They told him their story.

One night, they told him, they were on their way to Inverness from Strathspey to play in the streets when they were stopped on the road by an old man. He offered them a guinea apiece and as much whisky as they could drink if they would pipe for him and a few of his friends. This was a very good offer and they accepted at once.

The old man led them up the side of Tomnahurich. Halfway up the ancient, sacred mound they came across a great wooden door which the old man opened. They stepped inside to a great ballroom full of beautifully dressed, handsome men and women, all waiting to dance. They were given a dram, then another, and then they were ordered to play. As they did, the place came alive and all through the night the pipers played – refreshed with regular drams of the very finest whisky.

At last the dance came to an end and the old man thanked them, gave them a guinea each and led them to the door. It was then that they started to get worried: the city had changed suddenly and there were strange, hard, noisy beasts in the streets. They told the sheriff they had concealed their golden guineas from the police thus far, but now they handed them over to him only to watch the coins crumble into dust.

They were returned to the cells and a minister was called to have a word with them. One of them then told the clergyman that he had been at the Battle of Sherrifmuir (D35) the week before. The Battle of Sherrifmuir took place in the seventeenth century! At once the minister began to intone a prayer. As soon as the name of God was mentioned, the pipers, their pipes and clothes crumbled into a pile of dust around the minister's feet.

This story is told in many places in Scotland, sometimes with fiddlers instead of pipers, and it seems to combine a belief in the fairies with an ongoing respect for places of ancient sanctity, as well as providing a very good tale for a winter's night. Tomnahurich, though, was believed to be the main meeting place for the fairies in all of the Highlands which led to its alternative name, Tom na Sitheachan, the hill of the fairies. In some versions one of the musicians is smart enough to stick a knife or other iron object in the door of the fairy hill, thus ensuring his escape. (This because the fairies are said to come from a time before iron and therefore the metal acts as a countercharm to their wiles.)

## Calton Hill

Another famous fairy hill is Calton Hill overlooking Princes Street in the heart of Edinburgh (D56, 57).

Around the year 1660 a seaman called Captain Burton was witness to a remarkable event. He had been told of a young lad called the Fairy Boy who had the second sight. Burton was intrigued and arranged to meet the boy. The lad told the captain that every Thursday night he would take his drum to Calton Hill. There, a great pair of gates in the side of the hill would open. He would enter and play for the fairies as they danced through the night. There was a great deal of feasting and drinking and on occasion they would all fly off through the air to France or Holland and hold their revelry there. The Captain was sceptical, but the boy said he was bound to attend these celebrations every Thursday and that all of Scotland could not keep him away. Intrigued, Burton assembled a group of his friends the next

Thursday and they met the Fairy Boy in a hostelry. They intended to keep him in conversation until past his supposed appointed hour at which point they thought they would force him to confess to making it all up. But an hour before midnight they suddenly realised that he had managed to slip away from them. They rushed out into the night and headed towards the hill. They found the lad and dragged him back to the tavern, but within minutes he had gone again and this time could not be found. It was thought he had managed to go and join his fairy friends.

The Fairy Boy

Today, Calton Hill is also the site of Beltane rites and probably was at other significant times of the year in earlier centuries. Its name means 'hill of the hazels'. Hazel trees provided the nuts used in divination, particularly at Halloween, and in ancient belief in the Celtic-speaking world the hazel was a sacred tree, particularly its nuts. The Beltane festival on Calton Hill was accompanied by the Robin Hood Games – a day when all kinds of mischief took place, a celebration frowned on after the Reformation.

You can get a clear idea of what was going on from some of the characters involved in the games. One of the principal characters was the Abbot of Misrule and in the games Robin Hood and Little John were seen as representatives of the common people and would fight with bishops and noblemen. There was a considerable amount of drinking and general mayhem.

In the eighteenth century great religious gatherings with several preachers seem to have taken on some of the aspects of these more ancient assemblies, as can be seen from Robert Burns's poem 'The Holy Fair'. After the Reformation the Kirk decided to suppress the games themselves, but it took several years, fines and even imprisonment before the people gave up this ancient practice.

The revival of Beltane on such a site has a certain sense to it and its attraction can be seen in the ever-increasing number of young people and families who attend.

# The Fairy Hill of Aberfoyle

Aberfoyle (C11), in the heart of the magnificent Trossachs, has its own fairy hill which is the focus of a remarkable story.

In 1679 the local minister, Robert Kirk, published *The Secret Commonwealth of Elves, Fauns and Fairies*, an investigation into ancient beliefs among the Highland population. In this book he stated that many Highlanders believed that their ancestors' spirits lived in the fairy hills – a possibility remarkably close to what seems to have been the belief of the people who raised the chambered cairns thousands of years before – and that for every churchyard there would be a fairy mound where the souls of the dead might pass. There the souls would remain until the Day of Judgement. It was a matter of faith that no one should ever interfere with such mounds as this would displease the 'little people' and bring misfortune to anyone who disturbed them.

This amalgam of beliefs finds a strange echo in the fate of Reverend Kirk himself. Kirk was a seventh son and had been born with the gift of second sight – a talent which is seen as a curse as often as a blessing. All in all, the tone of *The Secret Commonwealth* and its great detail make it easy to believe that Kirk had a belief in 'the people of peace'. *The Secret Commonwealth* contains very detailed descriptions of the fairies and how they behaved, and local people believed that he had gone too far: the fairies were extremely displeased to have their secrets disclosed.

One day while he was walking on the fairy hill of Aberfoyle he fell down dead and local people said it was the work of the fairies. After his funeral his spirit came to a relative and told him that he was not dead but that he had been taken away to Fairyland. He asked him to pass on a message to another cousin, Graham of Duchray. The message was that at the forthcoming baptism of his son he would appear in the room. At that point Duchray was to throw the knife or dirk he held in his hand over the spirit's head and the spell would be broken and Kirk would return, alive. But, he said, 'If this be neglected, I am lost forever.'

The appointed day came and, true to his word, Kirk appeared.

His cousin Duchray was so astonished that he could not bring himself to throw the knife. The spirit of the lost minister disappeared and has never been seen since.

## The Two Hunchbacks

Near Kilchrenan (C23) by Loch Awe there is a fairy mound with an interesting tale. The story is known all over the world and I first heard it as a joke in a Dundee pub, which just illustrates how tenacious the ideas of our ancestors can be!

In a clachan near Kilchrenan there lived two hunchbacks, Hamish and Handy who, although going to the same school, having the same age and suffering from the same deformity, were like chalk and cheese. Hamish was a capable, kindly lad while Handy was an idle, worthless chiel with a wicked tongue. He took great delight in making Hamish miserable any chance he got.

Hamish was deeply in love with a lass called Morag, a local beauty, and when one day he realised this, Handy told everyone that such a beauty would have nothing to do with a deformed creature like Hamish. After finishing work that same day Hamish wandered off on his own and sat down on a hillside where he burst into tears. Suddenly he heard his name being spoken and

The two hunchbacks

looked up to see a small but beautiful woman dressed all in green. She asked what was wrong and he poured out his heart to her, telling her all about his feelings for Morag and his problems with Handy. The woman smiled and told him to come that night to a wee green knoll, to knock on the hill and say 'Fosgail an dorus' three times – 'Open the door'.

That night Hamish made his way to the knoll and, knocking gently on the hill with the stick he needed to help him walk, he said the magic words. At once a door opened and he stepped inside. He found himself in a large well-lit chamber full of the wee folk, with beautiful music filling the air. Seated on a dais in the centre of it all was the woman he had met earlier whom he now realised was the Queen of the Fairies herself. She explained that she had taken pity on him and asked if he would like her to cast a spell on Morag to make her love him. Hamish said no, he did not think it fair to have Morag fall for a wee twisted creature like himself.

'What would you have?' asked the queen.

'Make me like other men,' said Hamish, 'straight and tall.'

Hardly were the words out of his mouth when he found himself looking down at the little people: his hunchback had disappeared! The queen smiled and asked what he thought of his chances with Morag now. Hamish could hardly speak in his excitement and stammered that he would have to wait and see.

The very next moment he was outside the fairy hill and rushing home. His new appearance gave him new confidence and he went to Morag and told her how he felt. She saw before her a well-built handsome young man with a kindly air and a sparkle in his eyes and soon he was ahead of all her other suitors in her affections.

Handy was beside himself with jealousy when he saw what had happened and he came to Hamish demanding how he had managed to change himself. Despite Handy's past actions Hamish was never a lad to hold a grudge and freely told Handy what had happened, stressing that he must say the appropriate phrase only three times, no more no less. Handy immediately started planning for what he could do once he too had got rid of his hunchback.

That night, bursting with excitement, Handy approached the knoll. He stamped heavily on the wee hill, shouting out 'Fosgail an dorus' three times, then a few times more for good measure. In all he shouted it seven times.

Right enough the door opened and he was pulled in. But it was no scene of merriment and pleasure he found. The fairies were indignant and stood around him ominously. Handy looked at the queen but made no gesture of respect. He was asked what he wanted and he told them he wanted what Hamish had been given. At that point one of the fairies tweaked his coat and the head-strong Handy skelped him across the ear. Immediately he found himself birling through the air. The next thing, he was alone on the wee hillock with Hamish's hump on his back as well as his own.

When the story came out he was greatly pitied but many people could not help but laugh, and soon he was left to wander who knows where.

In time Morag agreed to be Hamish's wife and when they were married and raising a family they never passed the fairy hill of Kilchrenan without a good word or kind thought for the little people.

# CHAPTER 2

# The Goddess in the Landscape

ALL PAGAN RELIGIONS IN Europe have come through a 'goddess phase' and there is no reason to think Scotland should have been any different. Behind tales of witches, supernatural females and female saints lies a reality that is still manifest in our landscape – a goddess walked these lands, and perhaps still does. In ancient religions life was seen to emanate from a female source and the landscape of Scotland is dotted with references to the female principle in its nurturing, life-giving sense, though we also have dark, violent females suggesting the destructive aspect of a goddess, in short life and death.

Many of the most striking of our hills are called paps, and in Gaelic cioch and mam both refer to the differing shapes of the female breast. We have the Paps of Jura (C19), the Paps of Fife, the Pap of Glencoe (A23), the Maiden Paps (D65) in Roxburghshire, Maiden Pap (B6) in Sutherland and many others. There is also Bennachie (B44) (originally Bean na Cioch) and Lochnagar (B42), initially Beinn na Ciochan, with its own Caisteal na Caillich, Meikle Pap and Little Pap. There are many others, but the fact that they have been named after the shape of the female breast is perhaps not enough to conclude that we are seeing remnants of a goddess and her cult. However, when we find holy wells and symbolic placenames associated with ritual and mythology and early sacred sites around such places it seems possible that goddess worship was involved in the naming of such physical features.

The Cailleach

In many parts of Scotland that were once Gaelic-speaking – which is most of the country – there are tales of the Cailleach, a name meaning 'old woman' or 'hag'. In many of the old tales however she is presented as the Spirit of Winter, keeping Bride, the Goddess of Summer imprisoned until she is released by her lover. As we shall see, the Cailleach in Gaelic tradition is matched by the figure of the Carlin in Scots tradition. There are literally dozens of placenames referring to the Cailleach and many such tales are attached to mountains.

## The Cailleach

One of the oldest tales of this kind refers to Scotland's greatest natural wonder. This is the Corryvreckan (C17), a great whirlpool between the Inner Hebridean islands of Jura (C18) and Scarba. Just off Scarba's south coast there is a huge underwater spike and when the Atlantic waters are forced through the Sound of Jura and meet tidal surges coming around both islands the waters start to gyrate around this spike and the whirlpool Corryvreckan is formed. It is at its most violent at the end of autumn although sailors who dare to cross it are always in danger at any time of the year.

The name of the Corryvreckan comes from Coire Bhreacain, the cauldron of the plaid. The cauldron is associated with god-desses throughout Celtic and Germanic mythology and legend, which may be why it is represented so widely on Pictish symbol stones, but here it has a specific meaning. It was in this great caul-dron that the Cailleach washed her plaid, the traditional one-piece garment of the Highlands. It was this washing that was said to have created the whirlpool in autumn, the sound of which can be heard for many miles around. After washing her plaid the Cailleach is said to lay her plaid over the hills of west Scotland to dry. As she is the oldest being, her plaid is pure white – it needed no colour to differentiate her from other beings. This is, of course, a mythological explanation for the first snows of the year, linked to the greatest physical event in the landscape of Scotland and her surrounding waters. Some scholars link the Cailleach to Ben Nevis specifically. Like many of our hills it has an Allt na Cailleach, stream of the Cailleach.

This is essentially the same Cailleach located in different parts of Scotland, as in Caillich na Mointich, the Cailleach of the moors, whose form lies in the hills to the south of the great stone circle of Calanais which we shall look at later.

Time and again we find the Cailleach associated with mountains, and on a clear day as the weather changes it is easy to see why. I recall standing on a hillside in Glen Clova looking north to Lochnagar in early autumn on a bright day with a few clouds high in the sky. As I watched, clouds began to form around the head of Lochnagar and as the sky darkened clouds began to stream out from the mountain. A goddess, of course, creates the weather as well as the planet and all its beings and it seems only natural that she should be located on our mountain tops. The harsh black figures of the Cailleach associated with Bein Bhreac in Lochaber, Ben Wyvis (B10) in Easter Ross and many other Scottish mountains seem particularly apt creatures to be associated with Scottish winters which every year exact a toll of sacrifice from among the walkers and climbers who venture amongst them.

One of the strongest associations of the Cailleach is with the deer. Jura, mentioned above, means 'deer isle'. The Cailleach there, Cailleach Mhor nam Fiadh, big cailleach of the deer, is said to have no remorse in killing any non-Jura man who sets foot on her island. This is very close to the notion of a goddess representing the land, and connects to the Celtic idea of a new king marrying the female representation of the land and thereby attaining sovereignty. Many cailleachs are mentioned as helping deer hunters who approach them the right way.

Ben Cruachan (C24), which soars over the north side of the road between Dalmally and Oban, has its own Cailleach story. Here the Cailleach was the guardian of a well on the summit of the mountain. Every evening she had to cover the well with a large flat stone and every morning take it off again. One night she was tired out after being out all day with her herds in Connel and fell asleep by the side of the well. Night fell and still she slept. Up came the waters of the well and flooded out over the land, rushing down the side of the mountain to the south. As the flood began to rage it broke through the Pass of Brander with a great roar and the Cailleach sprang awake. Try as she might she could not cap the well and the torrent flowed free, drowning many a man and beast caught in its path. This is how Loch Awe was formed and it is said the Cailleach was so ashamed that she turned to stone and the stone still sits among the rocky ruins overlooking the Loch.

Here, as with the Corryvreckan, we have the Cailleach being instrumental in the formation of the landscape. The same story of the overflowing well has given us the origin of Loch Ness and other lochs. It is no surprise that tradition also tells us that the Cailleach formed the Western Isles when an apronful of stones she was carrying for the making of Scotland accidentally fell!

On Mull the Carn na Caillich (A21) is where the Cailleach dropped a load of stones when the strap of the creel she was carrying the stones in broke. She is said to have been trying to build a bridge over the Sound of Mull and intended to put chains across the Sound of Islay to stop ships passing.

The stone circle of Calanais laid out on the ground in the shape of a Celtic cross over five thousand years ago is truly one of Scotland's wonders. Its use in lunar observation is now accepted and in the hills along which the moon 'dances' at the end of its 18.6 year cycle we can see how important the notion of a goddess in the landscape must have been. In these hills to the south of the Calanais complex the outline of a reclining human figure can be seen. Though it is only recently that archaeologists have rediscovered the lunar associations of this magnificent megalithic site, local tradition has preserved at least one memory of the sanctity of the area. The term for the human figure reclining in the hills to the south is Cailleach na Mointich – Cailleach of the moors. In this case, the Cailleach may be a goddess, here present to underline the importance of the complex of megalithic sites around Loch Roag.

In a tale told all over the Highlands, the Cailleach – in this case, a great, black-faced hag – has Bride, the Goddess of Summer, imprisoned. In some versions they are mother and daughter. During the winter while Bride is imprisoned, the Cailleach goes around the country hammering the land with her great hammer and thus freezing it. Bride is given the impossible task of washing a brown fleece white while the Cailleach is out and about. Far off in the Land of Eternal Youth, Angus Og dreams of the beautiful maiden harshly imprisoned and resolves to come to her rescue.

Bride herself manages to escape on the 1st of February for three days but is soon recaptured. This is supposed to account for the three days of good weather that were said to happen at the beginning of February.

Meanwhile Angus Og searches everywhere for Bride, and with the help of a mysterious male figure eventually locates her. He frees her and the couple are initially pursued by the Cailleach. But with Bride's release spring has come and the Cailleach's powers fade quickly. At last she gives up the chase in disgust and throws her hammer under a holly bush – which is why nothing ever grows there. Bride and Angus Og are married and rule together over the summer months until once again the Cailleach's time comes round.

This tale comes from long before the calendars were changed at the end of the sixteenth century so it is perhaps surprising how a short spell of good weather does indeed occur at the beginning of February sometimes. Or did the new calendar simply put things back in balance?

## *The Carlin*

In the east of Scotland, Scots-speaking for almost as long as Gaelic has been spoken in the west, there is a figure who is a clear match for the Cailleach. This is the Carlin who, like her counterpart, has left traces in the landscape.

On the western side of the Lomond Hills, of which the Paps of Fife form part, is the narrow gap known as Glenvale. Here stood a striking pillar of stone known as Carlin Maggie, which sadly has now fallen. The tale is that this was a witches' haunt and Carlin Maggie was their leader. One time seeing Satan approach carrying a load of rocks she took a stand on Bishop's Hill (D40) and proceeded to flyte him – insult him in rhyme. He dropped his load of rocks and chased her, coming close enough to turn her into stone at a spot overlooking Loch Leven. Here we have a representative of the old, pagan religion going against even the Christian Devil! In the surrounding area there are records of fertility rituals associated with a nearby hole called the Maiden Bore (D41), old wells and even an early Christian 'fish' sign carved in the living rock on West Lomond Hill. The clustering of such sites strongly supports the idea that such names were given in honour of a goddess and that the area was one of considerable sanctity.

The Carlin was the subject of one early anonymous poem, 'The Gyre-Carling', in which she is said to have farted out North Berwick Law! The poem was said to have been a favourite of James V. This is a bit different from the other tales here but still links her directly to the creation of the physical world and it is interesting that one of our most famous groups of witches gathered in the shade of North Berwick Law (D54). The name Gyre-Carling means something like the biting or ravenous old woman, very like the meaning of the Cailleach Bheur, a name that crops up often in Gaelic tradition.

The Gyre-Carling in the poem is also remarkably like the Cailleach in the poem 'The Manere of the Crying of Ane Playe' by William Dunbar, the great fifteenth/sixteenth century poet. There, as the wife of Finn,

> She spittit Lochlomond with her lips;
> Thunner and fireflaucht flew fae her hips.

'Fireflaucht' is lightning and this may be a reference to her role as the source of storms and bad weather. The similarity between the Cailleach and Carlin here is absolute.

A striking suggestion of ancient worship and ritual comes from Loch Carlingwark (C2) in Dumfries and Galloway. Here in the loch a great collection of votive gifts was found – gifts put into wells, rivers or lochs accompanying prayers to a goddess, or perhaps a god. Among the collection from Carlingwark, to be seen the Museum of Scotland, is a great cauldron, echoing the relationship between many early goddess figures and the actual source of food for family and communities. Water has also long been central to pagan religion and accounts for the long association of prayer and ritual with wells, as we shall see later.

## Bride / St Brigit

One tale that occurs in several locations tells how on the morning of Beltane, the Cailleach went to a holy well. Taking a mouthful of water just as the sun rose, she drank and was magically transformed into the summer goddess, Bride, the possible forerunner of St Brigit who has long been revered in Ireland and Scotland. This story corresponds to the old notion of the year being split into two main seasons – the 'time of the Big Sun' and the 'time of the Little Sun'. These seasons were separated by the great feasts of Beltane and Samhain. Although the other great quarter-day feasts of Imbolc (1 February) and Lammas (1 August) were undoubtedly important they are clearly overshadowed by the other two. Imbolc itself is 'Bride's day' and was linked to the start of lambing.

St Brigit is essentially the Christianised version of an earlier goddess whose popularity in Ireland spread to Scotland. She may have been mother goddess of the Brigantes, a British tribe from present-day northwestern England. She is closely matched in Norse mythology by Freyja.

Brigit survives in Gaelic tradition as the birthmaid of Christ. As we shall see later, there are many Bride's Wells in Scotland and the number of Kilbrides shows the extent of churches once dedicated to her. However, there are other Brigit names that suggest a strong connection to the earlier goddess figure.

In Glen Clova in the Angus foothills of the Grampians there is a pool by the roadside just east of the Gella bridge called Bride's Coggie (a coggie is Old Scots for a wooden bucket). In the same area there are placenames which refer to women which might give more weight to the idea of a goddess site here. There is Clachnabrain which comes from the Gaelic Clach na Mnathan, the stone of the women, and Braeminzeon which is Braigh na Mnathan, hillside of the women. Near Bride's Coggie in the shadow of the Craigs of Lethnot was the first location of a church in the glen. In a story that is repeated throughout the country we are told that the stones of the church were always moved overnight from the selected spot until the site itself was changed. In a glen just a few kilometres to the east, Glenesk (D3), is Bride's Bed, which may refer to an ancient man-made circular depression below Craigmaskeldie (D2) at the head of the glen. Also in Angus is Bride's Ring (D17), the remains of a prehistoric defensive structure.

Several examples of the rituals associated with Bride and St Brigit have been described in the past. In the Western Isles where Bride's importance is emphasised in her title as 'handmaiden to Mary' or 'birthmaid to Christ', intricate procedures accompanied Imbolc. Old women would make an oblong basket in the shape of a cradle, which they would call leaba Bride, Bride's bed. They would then take pains to decorate it with primroses, daisies and other flowers that open their eyes in the morning of the year. These would have been gathered from sunny sheltered valleys nearby. After that they would take a sheaf of corn and fashion it into the shape of a woman which they would then dress up with brightly-coloured ribbons, sparkling sea shells and bright stones from the hill. When it was all dressed and decorated, one of the women would go to the door of the house and, standing on the step with her hands on the jambs, call quietly into the darkness, 'Bride's bed is ready.' Another woman behind her would reply, 'Let Bride come in. Bride is welcome.' Then the woman at the door would again address Bride: 'Bride, come thou in, thy bed is made. Preserve the house for the Trinity.'

With great ceremony the women would lay the figure of Bride in the bed. A small straight white wand (the bark having been peeled off) would then be placed beside the figure. These wands were generally of birch, broom, bramble, white willow or other sacred wood. The women would then level the ashes on the hearth, smoothing them over carefully. The following morning the whole family would make a close examination of the ashes. If they found the mark of the wand of Bride they would rejoice, but if what they found was lorg Bride, the footprint of Bride,

Bride

they would have cause for great celebration, for this was taken to mean that Bride herself was present in their home during the night. This was widely believed to mean that there would be increase in family, in flock and in field in the coming year. If there were no marks on the ashes, the family would be disappointed, for they thought that this was a sign that Bride was offended and had not heard their call. They would then make offerings to try and propitiate her. This is clearly nothing to do with Christianity, even if Bride was 'the birthmaid of Christ'.

Within Gaelic tradition there is one association with Bride that stands out as a particularly strong echo of pre-Christian thought and that is her association with the serpent. The serpent in Christian terms is of course evil, but several rhymes survive showing that Bride was directly associated with this unlikely creature. In Scottish terms the association is specifically with the adder, our only indigenous snake. It is also of course a creature strongly linked with various traditions regarding those most romantic and insubstantial figures, the druids. McNeill in *The Silver Bough* gives this version of a hymn to the adder which was believed to emerge from its hibernation on Imbolc (St Brigit's Day, or 1 February):

Today is the day of Bride.
The serpent shall come from the hole.
I will not molest the serpent
Nor will the serpent molest me.

This has been commented upon as a relic of serpent worship by several commentators but it is probably truer to say that the serpent/adder is a symbol associated with a mother goddess. The serpent has been seen by many cultures as a symbol of knowledge. The creature's habits of shedding its skin and of hibernating underground make it a good symbol for the ideas of regeneration and rebirth. In ancient times when prayers were said to try and ensure the harvest for the coming season, the serpent's association with the earth itself was also significant. There are scholars who think that our ancestors prayed to those who had gone before them to work magic on the seeds in the earth to ensure harvest the following year. The appearance of a variety of serpent/adder representations on Pictish symbol stones strongly suggests they saw it as a powerful religious symbol and not impossible that they associated it with Bride herself.

We should remember that these practices are recorded as happening in communities that had been ostensibly Christian for over a thousand years! The idea of Bride, an aspect of a mother goddess, continued to have a hold on both community and individual until very recently. Just as Bride is associated with the serpent, the Cailleach is associated with the cauldron (another symbol found on the Pictish symbol stones). As the passage above illustrates, there were also rituals associated with such figures – rituals that might come from as far back as the Stone Age.

# CHAPTER 3

# The Cateran

MANY WRITERS HAVE TOLD OF the bleak harshness of Rannoch Moor (c25), the windswept, boggy area of Scotland between Loch Rannoch and Glencoe. This is an area where the weather is harsh for much of the year, where there is little shelter and seemingly little life. Yet this apparently barren area is the site of stories that have been passed down by word of mouth, giving us a picture of a period of our history that has yet to be clearly understood.

For this is the area in the years after Culloden where the Cateran gathered. Cateran is a Gaelic word originally meaning warrior, but due to the habits and practices of ancient tribal warrior society in Scotland it has become linked to one activity specifically: cattle-raiding. From Iron Age times the warrior tribes of Britain counted their wealth in cattle, and even into the eighteenth century this ancient way of life survived, warriors proving themselves by lifting another clan's cattle. This was not considered theft; it was how the warriors showed their skill and courage and was particularly important for anyone who hoped to lead the clan. For we must remember that if a chief was not up to his job, clan society had ways and means of making sure someone else took his place. It is also true to say that the hereditary chief was not always the leader in battle. Rather, this was likely to be the role of the best or most skilful of the warriors of the clan, and owed as much to intelligence and creativity as to strength of arm.

## *Serjeant Mor*

The highland warriors who gathered in the autumn on Rannoch in the years after 1746 were the last remnants of a dying society. The smashing of the Jacobite army on Culloden Moor on 16 April that year was followed by widespread killings and repression throughout the Highland area. As often as not, other Scots were responsible for the slaughter and rapine, but they were without doubt following a government policy designed to eradicate independent clans for ever. The survivors of Culloden who gathered in Rannoch no doubt knew their days were numbered, but facing execution or exile, they had made their decision. By this period the traditional cattle-raiding had broken down and for a while many clans raided the more prosperous lowlands. Now they felt justified in taking cattle, and even the personal possessions of anyone who had supported the Hanoverian cause. Presbyterian ministers were a prime target in the late 1740s. The raids on the Lowlands over the previous half century and longer had led to a curious situation where some clansmen acted as guardians of cattle against other clans. It is one of the ironies of Scottish history that contracts of blackmail from these times have survived, revealing blackmail was as much a form of insurance as of extortion.

The men in Rannoch would raid anywhere they could. In response, the government had four- to twelve-man garrisons in every glen in Angus, Aberdeenshire, Inverness-shire, Perthshire, much of Sutherland and parts of Argyll. These garrisons were linked by mounted patrols but the Cateran were active until 1753

Sergeant Mor

when the most famous of them, Serjeant Mor, was hanged at Perth (82). In this period not only were the Highlanders banned from carrying their traditional weaponry of dirk, sword and pistols or musket, but the wearing of a kilt and the playing of bagpipes were also banned – except in those British army regiments which were formed from the 'loyal' clans.

Iain Dubh Cameron had served in the French army and when Prince Charles Edward Stewart raised the Jacobite Rebellion he resigned his post and came back to Scotland. A veritable giant of a man, the Serjeant Mor became the subject of many tales in the years after Culloden when the Cateran were hidden and made up by the Highland population – despite the presence and repressive activities of the British army. Surviving stories and situation reports from the garrisons themselves describe what we would nowadays call a guerrilla war. Not only was Serjeant Mor adept in the traditional art of cattle-lifting, he was a shining example of the Highland idea of honour.

One day somewhere in or near the Mamore range south of Ben Nevis, Serjeant Mor came across a mounted Englishman with a heavily laden pack horse. He addressed the man, politely noting that there was something of the military man about him though he was not wearing the red coat of the British army. Although initially alarmed at the sight of this big, traditionally dressed Highlander, the Englishman soon began to relax. He said he was heading for Fort William (A24), had lost his way and asked if he could be pointed towards the right road. Serjeant Mor offered to take him on his way. Delighted, the Englishman revealed that he had been very worried that he might be apprehended by the dreadful Serjeant Mor since he was the paymaster carrying all the soldiers' wages. The Highlandman rode alongside saying nothing as the man went on and on about monstrous Serjeant Mor, and the depredations he had been carrying out against man and beast throughout the Highlands. At last they came in sight of the road to Fort William.

At this the giant Highlander spoke. 'There is your way clear before you. As to what you say of the Serjeant Mor, it is all untrue. He is a soldier, not a thief. And apart from one sad occasion in

Strathspey, no-one but a soldier has ever died at the hands of him or his men.'

'How do you know this?' asked the Englishman.

'My name is Iain Dubh Cameron; I am the Serjeant Mor,' came the reply, 'There before you is the road to Inverlochy Castle; you cannot mistake it. You and your money are safe. Tell your governor in future to be sending a more wary messenger with his gold. You can tell him that although I am forced to live as an outlaw I am as much a soldier as he is and I would despise lifting his gold from a defenceless man who confided in me.'

At that the Highlander turned his horse and headed back into the hills leaving a flustered, dumbfounded but heartily relieved paymaster to gallop into Fort William.

After seven years of dodging the troops and supplying a butcher in Perth with a constant supply of fresh meat (to mutual advantage), Serjeant Mor was at last caught at Dunan, just to the east of Rannoch Moor. Already several of his companions had been caught and hanged, but his own capture had required treachery: he had been sold out by one he considered a friend. That so-called friend was made to quit Scotland soon after by the force of local opinion.

To the last Serjeant Mor kept his dignity, never changing his position that he was a soldier in the army of the legitimate heir to the throne. When he was eventually tried and found guilty in Perth, the court still had the ancient office of doomster. His role was to come to court once a sentence of death was passed and place his hand on the head of the prisoner to intimate that his fate was now sealed. As Cameron was sentenced to death by hanging the judge rang a small bell and the black-clad doomster entered and approached the prisoner. Despite being heavily chained, Serjeant Mor struggled to his feet and straining mightily, freed an arm.

'Keep that caitiff [fool] off me. Let him not be touching me or I will give him a terrible skelp,' roared the irate giant.

The doomster fled the court in terror but nothing could prevent the sentence being carried out. On 23 November 1753 Serjeant Mor was hanged at the Burgh Muir in Perth. After this the Highlands were quiet.

## Cam Ruadh

On the A93, the road from Blairgowrie to Braemar, there is a dangerous turn overhanging a sheer drop, generally known as the Devil's Elbow. Overlooking the road to the west is the mountain Cairnwell (D9), which gave its name to the pass. The old stagecoach to Braemar used to stop here at a spot known as Kateran's Howe. Passengers would have seen fourteen mounds in the howe, or hollow. These were the graves of raiders from Argyll killed in the mid-seventeenth century Battle of Cairnwell, the largest of which was over two metres long, said to be that of a chieftain of the MacDairmaid sept of Clan Campbell. This was John Grant, known as Cam Ruadh, which translates as something like Twisted Red. For generations after his death his birthplace was said to be either Glen Taitnach off Glenshee (D5) or Alltnahait in Glen Clunie (B41). This rivalry led to many disputes and some blood being spilt by inhabitants of both places.

Cam Ruadh was well-named. He was little more than five feet tall, stockily built with bow legs and flat feet. His broad flat face had a pug nose and beady eyes, his cheeks were red and blotchy with protuberant veins. Below each eye his cheekbones jutted out crudely and his face was covered in thin straggly red bristles. His one good eye was of a brilliant blue but the other was an opaque horror, streaked with red and permanently open. His lips were thin, barely covering his uneven, squint teeth. All of this was topped off by an unruly thatch of coarse red hair said to resemble nothing so much as a hedgehog.

His voice was thin and squeaky, and he was stubborn, quick-tempered and possessed of a truly waspish tongue. He was as cunning as a fox and as tenacious as a bulldog. Despite this, he had married young and it seems was good husband. He was also phenomenally strong, without match as a runner in both speed and stamina, and though an excellent swordsman his greatest skill was with the bow. It is told of him that with his one good eye he could see a bluebottle on grey stone at twenty yards and hit it with one shot. No one in living memory had ever shot an arrow more than half as far as Cam Ruadh and it was said he could hit a

Cam Ruadh

midgie or fell an ox with a single arrow. With these skills he was a valued member of his clan and often involved in the fights and skirmishes that often accompanied cattle-raiding.

When pursuers caught up with raiders, sometimes the matter was settled by means of single combat, sometimes by battle between pre-selected numbers and occasionally by wholesale fighting. The Battle of Cairnwell, triggered by the Argyll men lifting cattle from Glen Isla and Glenshee, was one of the latter.

As usual the cattle had been lifted during the night and when the theft was discovered in the morning the men from Isla and Glenshee gathered to give chase, sending a messenger off to Braemar for further help as it seemed the cleansers, as raiders were often called, seemed to be numerous. But then a dispute broke out about who had the right to lead the chase and the Glenshee men set off by themselves, followed by the Glen Isla men at a distance. Cam Ruadh stood back from all discussion: he had taken an oath the day before not to draw a bowstring for twenty-four hours, for it is said that he was growing sick of killing.

The Glenshee men ran off after the reivers and came up with them in the Pass of Cairnwell. Leading them was the Glenshee smith and his seven stalwart sons. They pressed ahead and attacked the Argyll men on their own as the Glen Isla men looked on from a nearby ridge. Heavily outnumbered they fell one by one and as each one fell the smith cried, 'Fight today, lads. Grieve tomorrow,' until at last he was cut down. He looked around in vain for the men from Braemar as one of the Argyll men came forward to finish him off. It was noon and the sun shone straight above him. The reiver lifted his sword to send the smith to join his sons and there was a twanging sound followed by a dull thud as the Argyll man was transfixed by an arrow. The smith breathed his last, smiling.

Cam Ruadh had watched in grief as his friends died but with the coming of noon his vow was over and he could join the fray. He had crept quietly behind a stone overlooking the Argyll men as arrow after arrow fell among them, each one finding its mark.

The men from Cromar were in turmoil – where was the mysterious bowman? The rain of death continued until a dozen men lay dead or dying including their mighty chieftain. Then a gust of wind lifted a corner of Cam Ruadh's plaid and the cleansers charged towards him. His bowstring snapped and Cam Ruadh cursed, throwing his bow at the approaching warriors. He turned and ran uphill. Several of his pursuers fired at him but with their friends in their line of fire they soon stopped.

The distance between them grew and, try as they might to speed up, the man before them drew away. One of the leading Argyll men knelt and took aim. The arrow fled true and thudded into John Grant's back. A cheer went up among the Cromar men but it choked back as they saw him continue running up hill as if nothing had happened. Within seconds he was out of bowshot. Another cheer rang out from the Glenshee men still battling in the pass.

It was answered by another from Meall Ordhar. The Braemar men had arrived! At this the onlookers from Glen Isla joined in and began to charge towards the men from Argyll. Realising they were seriously outnumbered they turned and fled, leaving the lifted cattle they had fought so hard to defend behind them.

It was a great victory but one fought at a terrible price. The Braemar men were hard put to prevent the Glenshee men from spilling the blood of the contingent from Glen Isla. Cam Ruadh silently took all the congratulations but refused all help, the shaft still sticking out from his shoulder. A few hours later they came home and as they passed through the glen several women shouted to Cam Ruadh that he had an arrow in his back, to which he replied every time, 'I know that myself already.'

On reaching his own croft the wee man sat on a stool and told his wife to pull the arrow from his back. She tugged and tugged, with never a sound from her man. But the arrow would not budge so he lay flat on his face and his wife stood on his back, a foot on either side of the shaft. At his word she bent and pulled with all her might. Out came the arrow with a lump of her husband's flesh. His wife then bound up the wound and Cam Ruadh proceeded to have a vast meal of venison, which all the Highlanders believed could do them nothing but good.

The Battle of Cairnwell had repercussions. The leader of the Argyll MacDairmaids had left seven young sons behind him on this raid and they vowed revenge. Several tales survive about the MacDairmaids' seeking revenge but the superior cunning of Cam Ruadh triumphed – until one year the Argyll lads decided to come after him in the middle of winter.

The story goes that Cam and his wife were sitting snug in their house while a vicious blizzard whirled outside. Mrs Grant said to her husband, 'What would you do, husband, if the Argyll men came after you on a night like this?'

'I would let them in by the fire and give them meat.'

'And then what would you be doing?' she asked.

'I think I would let them sleep through the worst of the storm.'

'And what then?'

'Och, I would let them be gone once the storm had passed.'

'Be as good as your word then,' came a gruff and quivering voice from outside, 'for we are close to death out here.'

'Surrender your arms first,' shouted Cam Ruadh, grabbing his sword and dirk and standing beside the door, back to the wall.

'Send your wife to the door and we will give her our weapons,' came the voice.

Mrs Grant went and opened the door and one by one the near-frozen MacDiarmaids handed over their weapons. A couple of them had to be carried by their brothers and the miserable group huddled round the roaring fire with hardly a glance at their intended victim. A sheep was butchered and put into the pot while the unexpected visitors were given bannocks and cheese, washed down with a bladder full of whisky. When the sheep was cooked all were fed and allowed to stay until the blizzard blew itself out. Having taken meat under Cam's roof the MacDiarmaids were under the obligations of hospitality and could do no harm to their host. Furthermore, so taken were they by his generosity and the realisation that he could have left them outside to die that the MacDiarmaids declared an end to the feud. In fact, they swore a bond of friendship and in future years were able to call upon the great military skills of Cam Ruadh in battles back in Argyll.

## Ledenhendrie

The traditional cattle-raiding of the Highland warriors was usually carried out on long autumn nights when the moon was full. There was no point in raiding a nearby clan – that would be too obvious and would lead to all-out war. Far better to show your mettle by raiding a good distance away where, if you were skilful enough, you might come back with a substantial haul. Such raiding was so central to the Highland way of life that there were set amounts to be paid for crossing other clans' lands with lifted cattle. In some cases these fees would ensure that the beneficiaries could refuse to let any pursuers chase raiders over their land.

By the seventeenth and eighteenth centuries Highland society was in decline and raids were beginning to be carried out in the Lowlands and as far away as Galloway. It seems likely that this type of activity had been an intrinsic part of society for centuries.

Year after year, raiders would follow established routes to prey on clans who in turn would attempt to prey on them. The routes in many instances are similar to the later drove roads, although the necessity for hiding from followers would take the reivers into more difficult and sheltered terrain. One route used by the Lochaber men for centuries was known as Rathad nam Marlach, or thieves' road, which name is perhaps not that old. The route came from Lochaber through Rothiemurchus, along the south side of the lovely Loch Morlich (B31), through the pass of Lochan Uaine (B30) by Loch Gamhna, then along the south side of Loch an Eilean (B32), then east into the hills. This route was extensively used at different times by men from the MacPherson, Cameron and MacIntosh clans and others from Badenoch and Strathspey.

In the lonely hills between Glen Clova and Glenesk there is an unassuming ridge overlooking the Water of Saughs (D6) called the Shank of Donald Young. This name commemorates a battle between raiders from Braemar and the men of Fern in Strathmore sometime around the beginning of the eighteenth century. The raiders had come into Strathmore and lifted all the cattle and other beasts around Fern, a wee village on the braes of Angus, about ten kilometres north of Forfar. As usual the raid took place in the dark and the raiders drove their booty up through Glen Lethnot (D7) and along the Water of Saughs, heading back towards Deeside. At dawn the loss was discovered and all the men from the surrounding area came into the village. Not all were keen to pursue the raiders, who were surely heavily armed and used to battle – most of the Fern men were farmers or crofters and had not been brought up to fight. Still, a couple of local men were keen on preserving Highland warrior traditions and gave the lead.

These men were James Winter, whose descendants lived on the braes of Angus until recently and James MacIntosh, better known as Ledenhendrie, the name of his farm, east of Fern. Both were skilled swordsmen and soon rallied a sufficient number of men, some equipped with firearms, to start the pursuit. A few hours later they caught up with the raiders two or three kilometres beyond Blackhaugh at the head of Glen Lethnot. As they neared the men driving the cattle, most of the raiders turned and came towards the Fern men, led by a veritable giant of a man. This was a weel-kennt reiver who had adopted the name of one of history's most notorious cattle-lifters, the Halkit Stirk. This is Scots for 'white-faced steer'.

The two sides faced each other and the giant issued a challenge that he would fight their best swordsman, and the winner take all. Both Ledenhendrie and Winter felt themselves bound by the code of Highland honour and Ledenhendrie accepted the challenge. The two men were not long fighting when it became obvious that the reiver had more than a height and reach advantage. He was also a very fine swordsman and laughingly sliced the buttons of MacIntosh's coat, calling on him to yield. Ledenhendrie was nothing if not courageous and would not surrender.

The two groups faced each other over open ground, the two swordsmen half way between them. Suddenly a hare started from the heather in front of the Fern men and made a beeline for the Highlanders. One of them immediately shouted (in Gaelic): 'It's a witch! They're using witchcraft!'

Ledenhendrie

Putting his gun to his shoulder, he fired at the speeding animal. He missed, but the Fern men, thinking he was breaking the agreement, immediately started to return fire. As the Fern men outnumbered the raiders by more than two-to-one, they soon had the better of the fight. Winter hamstrung the giant from behind but he continued fighting on his knees until he was killed by Ledenhendrie. Only the few Deeside men who had stayed with the cattle escaped. The cattle were recaptured. Of the Fern men only one, Donald Young, was killed and the ridge above where he died was given his name.

# CHAPTER 4

# The Turn of the Seasons

SCOTLAND STILL HAS FIRE rituals whose origins go back further than we know. The Burnin o the Clavie at Burghead (B21), the fireballs at Stonehaven (B46) and the dramatic Up-Hellya Festival in Shetland (B8) all celebrate the new year. In the past, however, there were many other seasons when the use of fire was central to ritual.

## *Beltane*

Midsummer Day, or St John's Day, was accompanied by bonfires, as were the two main festivals of the ancient agricultural year, Beltane and Samhain. These two festivals were the pivots of the year for most people in pre-industrial Britain. Beltane on 1 May was essentially a celebration of the summer and Samhain on 1 November was in some senses a feast of thanksgiving after the harvest was in. However there was much more to these great festivals and Beltane in particular has left many markers in the landscape.

Early commentators, misreading the first part of 'Beltane' interpreted it as a reference to the pagan Baal from the Bible. Others saw this central role of fire as a reference to a sun god – but things were hardly that simple.

In traditional Beltane celebrations, fires were lit on hilltops, which made them more visible. Several Scottish placenames mention fire for this reason. The dominating hill of Tinto (D64) in Lanarkshire was the site of the ancient fires, its earlier name Tintock deriving from Gaelic teinteach, fiery. There is another Tintock (C8) northeast of Glasgow. Carntyne (C6) derives from carn teineadh, or fire cairn, and between Teviotdale and Liddesdale is Needslaw, named after the neid-fire raised there. Another possible site name is

Beltane

Dundee, which some locals in the nineteenth century saw as being derived from deagh, meaning fire. Dundee Law (D18), like many ancient sacred hills, has a pronounced conical shape which might owe something to human intervention. The traditional processions of the ancient holy days were always deasail, literally 'sunwise', or clockwise, and Dundee Law has a road which follows a circular sunwise route to the top. Its position overlooking the Tay Basin, much of Fife and the Angus plain would ensure that a fire on its summit would be seen over a very wide area. Many Scottish hilltop sites, almost always interpreted as hillforts due to historians' militaristic cast of mind, have clumps of vitrified stone – stone melted together by extremely fierce heat. It is worth considering whether the use of such sites in quarterly fire rituals may have played a part.

In any case, it is certain that even into the nineteenth century many, if not most, parishes in Scotland seem to have had their own local, smaller hilltop sites for Beltane. One such place is Tully-belton (82) in Perthshire which does not have a particularly notable hill in the immediate area. Instead, Beltane fires were kindled at the circle of eight stones close by, just as was done at Calanais in Lewis and the Ring of Stenness in Orkney. Other places with obvious locations are Balquhidder (C15) and Killin (C16), both in Perthshire. At Balquhidder there is a small green conical hill which, like the one in Killin, known as Tom nan Ainneal, are quite likely to have been partially sculpted if not entirely raised by human hand. Even Iona, that example of Christian sanctity, has its Cnoc nan Ainneal, again meaning hill of fires. These neid-fires were created by friction because there could be no use of iron – flint and steel were prohibited. This is reminiscent of the avoiding of iron because the fairies 'disliked' it.

It was after the Beltane ceremony that cattle were taken to the high pastures to be fattened up, having been indoors for all of the winter and possibly much of the spring. (Today we tend to see things as either sacred or profane but in ancient times it is likely that such practicalities could easily be incorporated into practices we would see as primarily religious, or certainly spiritual. When one recalls that the Beltane fires were made in many cases from sacred woods which included such pungent materials as juniper, it could be there was an aspect of fumigation in this rite.)

Before the fire was ceremonially kindled, every hearth fire in the community was smoored. Once the main ceremonies were over each person would take a lighted piece of peat or a torch from the fire and return home. Then they would walk clockwise round their own lands and houses carrying the holy fire before entering the house to light the fire anew. This process of walking round the fields was known as saining. It combines the ideas of purification and sanctification – ensuring prosperity and good crops for the coming year.

The Beltane feast was a time for celebration which included the cooking of special foods. According to a report from Callander (C12) in the beautiful Trossachs, the Beltane ceremony was quite elaborate. The young men of each hamlet would meet on a hill and cut a round table in the ground, big enough for everyone involved to sit around it. They would make a fire and then a big dish of 'caudle' was made. This was a form of custard made from eggs and milk. They would also make the simple and delicious oatcakes known as bannocks. The Beltane bannock was special, however: it would be marked into portions, one for everyone in the company. Then one of these would be blackened with charcoal from the fire, broken into pieces and put into a bonnet or bag. The young men would all put on blindfolds and select a piece of bannock. The person who got the marked piece was then the 'devoted' one and made to jump three times through the flames. There is little doubt that this is an echo of a much earlier practice where the person chosen was actually sacrificed, quite probably by being burned alive. (Being chosen as a sacrificial victim was a great honour in ancient times.) And even more recently, there are hints in some reports that if anyone was injured or killed during the festivities of

Beltane or Samhain that this, though regrettable, brought good luck for the coming year. (After all, good luck was the primary reason for these festivals – to ensure the continuing turn of the seasons and the health of the crops and animals.) In some areas the chosen person was known as the cailleach bealtine and a great show would be made of pretending to throw the victim onto the fire.

Numbers were very important in the rituals and in most cases people would go three times round the fire. However, in some cases the number nine was of the greatest significance. In some Highland districts the raising of the neid-fire involved the number nine. A well-seasoned plank of oak would be bored through, into which hole would be placed a wimble or bore of the same wood. Sometimes a frame would be erected and in the middle an axle-tree would be fitted. Then nine people would turn it at a time. Sometimes as many as eighty-one people would be involved. The turning of the wimble in the wood, through the use of an axle-tree or not, created friction which caused heat, eventually raising a flame which would be fed with tinder to achieve a good flame. It was believed in most areas that if any of those turning the wood for the neid-fire were guilty of a serious crime then the fire would not start. As all the fires in the area or parish would have been smothered before the ceremony, it was vitally important that the ritual was successful. Until the nineteenth century certain local families were known for being 'of the stones' and tradition says that they had the duty of raising the neid-fire at the Beltane ceremonies held there.

It seems likely that this aspect of the ceremonies arose after the witch persecutions of the sixteenth and seventeenth centuries, while the rest of the rites come from much earlier.

Many of the customs associated with Beltane such as 'maying' – going to the woods to collect greenery – were not concerned with fertility in the abstract alone. This was customarily the time for a great deal of sexual activity.

Beltane feasts seem to have persisted longest in rural districts but it is in the city that they are being revived. For several years now the Beltane fires have blazed again on Calton Hill (as discussed above) and they have found an echo in various other places in

Scotland. The displacement of the Samhain fire feast to Guy Fawkes Night has kept certain aspects of that ancient feast of the dead alive.

On the south side of Kinnoull Hill (D23), Perth, overlooking the River Tay, there is a small cave known as the Dragon's Hole. This was the site of a particular Beltane rite until the end of the sixteenth century. An eyewitness account from 1559 tells of a strange flower-bedecked man standing at the cave entrance and repelling a series of young men who came up the hill to struggle with him. This rite drew virtually the entire populace from Perth and the eyewitness was told it commemorated the battle between St Serf and a dragon (which had preyed on the local lassies until the saint killed it). After the Reformation it took many years for the local presbytery to stop people going to celebrate this rite. There are records of fines being levied on such people and even today there are hearts scratched on the walls of the cave, suggesting that the link with fertility has not quite gone.

## Samhain

Samhain is the polar opposite of Beltane. Where Beltane is a feast of supplication, Samhain is in many ways a feast of thanksgiving. However, it does have a sense of ancestor worship and echoes of a cult of the dead.

The rituals of Halloween might go as far back in time as the Stone Age when the great chambered cairns of Scotland were built. People held on to these ancient beliefs to such an extent that in 835 the Church moved the Feast of All Saints from 21 February to 31 October to try and counteract the ancient pagan rituals. It did not work totally, however, as 2 November was consecrated in 998 as the Feast of All Souls, dedicated to the faithful dead of the Church.

All over Scotland the Samhain rites continued – and some still do. Around 1840 a Sheriff Barclay travelled from Dunkeld (D27) to Aberfeldy (D28) – no more than sixteen kilometres – and saw at least thirty fires blazing on hill-tops. He said that each had people dancing around it.

As at Beltane many of the rituals of Halloween involved repeating actions three or nine times but at this time of the year much of the activity centred round divination. While in ancient times this probably was a very serious business indeed, by historical times much of what was done had more to do with affairs of the heart than anything else.

Many of the sites of the Beltane fires were also used at Samhain as, for example, Calton Hill. Here the hazel trees which give the hill its name provided nuts which were used in the divination process. Two nuts would be placed on a shovel in the fire and if they jumped together this was a sign of good fortune in love, while if they jumped apart it signified heartbreak. Such was the extent of this practice that another name for Samhain or Halloween was Nutcrack Night.

Again, as at Beltane, special foods were prepared for Halloween. A very strange rite concerning the Halloween bannock used to take place just before Halloween in Rutherglen (c5) as late as the early nineteenth century.

The basic bannock was a sour type of cake whose dough had to be started over a week before they were needed. A group of six or eight women would gather in one house and mark out a sacred space in which to carry out their duties. There they would sit in a circle round the fire, each of them with a baking board on her knees. The leading figure was given the name Bride and the rest were designated her maidens. Two other women were called Hodler and Todler, the former on the eastern side of Bride, the latter on her other side. Todler would start by taking a small piece of the fermented dough and fashioning it into a bannock. She would pass it on to the person sitting next to her 'sunwise', or clockwise, who would work it more – and so it would go until the bannock was smooth and wafer thin at which point Bride would bake it on a griddle over the fire. The sitting in a circle, the passing of the bannock sunwise and the designation 'Bride' suggest a very old idea indeed. We recall that it is at Halloween that Bride, the Goddess of Summer, ends her reign and is replaced by the Cailleach, the Goddess of Winter.

In many parts of the country well into this century the idea of

Halloween fire was closely linked to the idea of witches. Young men in rural areas would go round the houses asking for peat to burn the witches. After dark the young folk would run around the fires shouting, 'Fire, fire. Burn the witches!' When the fires eventually died down the ashes would be scattered over a wide area to scare off all evil spirits – and incidentally to help fertilise the fields. When the last spark died, the gathered throng scattered with cries of 'Deil tak the hindmaist,' or even, 'The cutty black sow wantin a tail, tak the hindmaist!' (This might be a faded echo of the old association of the sow with goddess figures, noted by scholars. The association was always a dark one.)

Then the ashes of the fire would be laid out in the form of a circle and everyone present would place a stone round the edge of the circle. Whoever's stone was gone in the morning would not be expected to live out the year.

Witch-burning survived at Balmoral (B45) and Queen Victoria herself was supposed to have greatly enjoyed the spectacle. Here a figure of a witch called the Shandy Dann was brought to a great bonfire in a cart

Samhain

accompanied by pipers and others in traditional Highland dress. One brave soul would actually be in the cart with the dummy. As the procession came near the fire those pushing it would speed up, racing by the time they got there. Suddenly they would stop a few paces away from the fire. An indictment of the witch would be read out. Then, to the sound of skirling pipes, the cart would be rushed into the bonfire and tipped into it, the occupant of the cart leaping clear at the last possible moment. Like many of the rites of Halloween there seems to be some sort of memory of human sacrifice in this peculiar practice.

One of the trademarks of Halloween is, of course, dressing up.

Although this has now been superceded by the commercial practise of 'trick or treat', the tradition of guising at Halloween was originally more than just children having a laugh.

The idea of guising was to make oneself unrecognisable. It often involved cross-dressing. Guisers may have originated as pagan priests who represented the spirits of the dead. But ultimately, the disguise was to protect oneself from the attentions of the spirits who were believed to be abroad on the night as much as to provide a cover for mischief. It was long believed that the gap between the world of the living and the world of the dead shrank on Halloween when the dead and all sorts of spirits walk the earth.

The use of neep-lanterns (lanterns made from turnips) is traditional in Scotland, as opposed to pumpkins. Turnips introduce a haunting skull shape. This may hark back to the warrior tradition of collecting the skulls of enemies slain in battle. We know also that skulls were once used to decorate temples throughout Europe. And in Scotland there are wells all over with legends of people being beheaded and their heads then being washed there.

There are quite a few of these wells in Skye and even a Loch nan Ceann, loch of the heads, near Cuidrach (A18) in the Trotternish area of Skye. The story here is that in a battle between MacDonalds and MacLeods the former were totally victorious, killing all their enemies. They then cut their heads off and rolled them down a hill into the loch. As the heads rolled down the hill they were said to have called 'Theb, theab a latha dhol leinn,' – 'Almost, we almost won the day'. Many scholars see the idea of a head cult as in some way essentially Celtic but we should remember that in Norse mythology Odin himself cuts off the head of the giant Mimir, cures it in herbs and keeps it in Mimir's Well at the foot of the word-tree Yggdrasil.

An old name for the Halloween fire was 'shannack' and the night itself was sometimes known as Shannack Night. The term comes from Gaelic samhnach and survives in some placenames as, for example, Shannacher, near Fowlis Wester (D34), a wee village just east of Crieff in Strathearn. Here the link with the distant past is manifestly clear in the landscape. In and around Fowlis Wester there are standing stones, a stone circle, a Pictish cross-slab and an old kirk, showing the continuous of use of the area as a focus for religious behaviour from pagan through to Christian times. Our ancestors found certain places particularly well suited to religious observance and it is remarkable how many such sites still attract worshippers today.

Again a very wide spread practice was the raising of bonfires at Midsummer, renamed St John's Day in Christian times. The summer solstice has long been seen as a special day in most societies. So, too, in Durris (B47) on the river Dee near Banchory where the fires were lit on Cairnshee, the cairn of the fairies, and were supported by a bequest from a local man who left money for the local herd-boys to continue this festive rite.

CHAPTER 5

# Saints

It was deliberate Christian policy to take over pagan sanctuaries and build churches there as Pope Gregory wrote in the seventh century: 'In this way we hope that all the people, seeing that their temples are not destroyed, may abandon their error and, flocking more readily to their accustomed resorts, may come to know and adore the true God.' Churches are commonly found on top of mounds today, as St Vigean's (D12) at the edge of Arbroath. The overlap of pagan and Christian continued with religious leaders.

Scotland has many saints who do not figure in the official lists. Some do, of course, like Columba – but even he is associated with behaviour and attributes that hardly suggest Christian devotion. Some of our saints like St Brigit are clearly christianised versions of earlier pagan figures and yet others like St Kentigern seem to bridge the gap between pagan and Christian. There are saints who slay dragons in what might be allegories of the conquering of pagan belief, saints whose association with ancient holy wells helped to perpetuate the functioning of such sites and still other saints who seem to be pagan ambassadors.

The function of these saints' Lives seems to have been to convince people that the priests of the Church were more than a match for the pagan priests or druids who preceded them.

## St Serf

St Serf or St Servanus, as he was also called, is a mysterious figure. Of the many miracles attributed to him, one has it that he threw his pastoral staff across the River Forth from his cell at Culross (D38) and when it landed it took root and blossomed into an apple tree. Given the Celtic idea of Avalon (the Island of Apples) where Morgan took the wounded Arthur to be tended by her and her eight sisters, this idea is suggestive.

Serf

What St Serf is best known for, however, is his dragon-slaying. At Dunning in Strathearn he killed a dragon and is said to have done the same thing at the Dragon's Cave on the south side of Kinnoull Hill, Perth. He had been summoned to rid the country-side of the dragon that had been seizing maidens and taking them to his lair to devour them. This was the event said to be celebrated at the Dragon's Cave on Beltane up to the Reformation and beyond. This celebration obviously had to do with fertility. The eyewitness account we have describes the main participant being bedecked in flowers and greenery. This finds an echo in the festival of St Serf which used to take place in Culross on 1 July. This involved the carrying of tree branches and flowers as well as sacred relics and was accompanied by dancing and other revelry. The minute-book of the local kirk-session at Perth refers to 'hea-thenish practices' and describes young men and women marching to the Dragon's Hole with pipes and drums. They persisted for at least twenty years after the Reformation. In the cave mentioned above, there are hearts carved on the walls still – some traditions just quietly live on!

St Serf is also associated with the Culdees, successors of the Celtic church who practised alongside their Roman brethren in many of our great cathedrals into the Middle Ages. It was in his supposed capacity as a Culdee that Serf was given the large flat island in Loch Leven (D39) that still bears his name. Although he has wells and churches dedicated to him from Culross to Dunning and Dysart (D53), near Kirkcaldy, there is no real suggestion of when he lived other than his involvement with another saint, Kentigern.

## St Kentigern

Better known by the name Mungo, which was given him by St Serf, this early saint is a complex figure. As the patron saint of Glasgow he is especially associated with Glasgow Cathedral (C7). The Glasgow coat of arms shows a salmon and a ring that come from the best-known of his miracles.

St Mungo was at the court of the king of Strathclyde when the queen began to have an affair with one of the members of the court. Stupidly she gave him a ring which she had been given by the king himself. One day her lover was sound asleep by the side of the Clyde when the king came by and noticed the man wearing his ring. Carefully he slipped it from the sleeper's finger and threw it far out into the Clyde. Returning to the court he publicly asked the queen to bring him the ring he had given her. She immediately went to Kentigern to ask him what to do. He told her to send her handmaiden to the river with a net and bring back a salmon. The queen ordered this done and when the handmaiden returned with a salmon, Kentigern cut open the fish and there in its belly was the ring. The queen at once cleaned it and took it to her husband, who was forced to accept her pleas of innocence.

This looks suspiciously like a priest condoning adultery, but it may simply be a christianized version of an older story. For Kentigern seems to belong to an older world even though he is said to have met Columba (who came to Scotland from Ireland in 563). Kentigern's mother was Thenaw, daughter of King Loth of the Lothians. In the Arthurian romances he is portrayed as King Arthur's brother-in-law, and father of both Mordred and Gawain. Loth's capital was on Traprain Law, the massive hill that rises from the plain of East Lothian near Haddington (D5), the historical home of the Celtic tribe the Romans called Votadini.

His mother, Thenaw, was a devoutly Christian young woman who was determined to take a vow of chastity. Because of her innocence of all worldly matters she was seduced by a visiting prince who was young enough not to have yet grown a beard and passed himself off initially as a girl. Finding herself pregnant, the young girl informed her father. He flew into a rage but said it would all be made well if she married the beardless youth. She refused and in his anger the king then demanded she marry a lowly shepherd. When she refused yet again he ordered her to be put into a chariot and rolled off the top of Traprain Law. As the chariot went over the edge the maiden began to pray and instead of plummeting like a stone the chariot began to float gently downwards. This only served to make Loth even angrier and he decided she should be put to sea in a coracle with no oars. This was then done and she floated out on the tide into the Firth of Forth. Again she prayed and her coracle fetched up on the Isle of May (D52). From here she was accompanied by a vast shoal of fishes up the river and eventually landed at Culross on the northern bank of the Forth. Here she managed to light a fire and later gave birth to her son all alone. At that point St Serf came to investigate the light and finding the mother and child, the young Mungo / Kentigern, he took them into his community. Nothing more is told of Thenaw although St Enoch's bears a version of her name in Glasgow today.

Kentigern

Not only are St Mungo's antecedents straight from the oral tradition of Brythonnic-speaking Celtic tribes, some of the miracles attributed to him are redolent of magic and paganism. Perhaps due to the strangeness of his birth, Mungo was not popular with the other pupils of St Serf.

On one occasion it was his turn to sit by the fire to make sure it did not go out overnight but he fell asleep. Some of the other boys came upon him and smothered the fire. When he awoke the boy was faced with a cold fire in mid-winter. So he gathered up some leaves, prayed and blew on them and they burst into flame. The leaves he used are said to have been from the hazel tree, one of the ancient sacred woods often used in the raising of the neid-fire.

Another time when his back was turned the other boys killed St Serf's pet robin. He took the creature into his hands, said a prayer over it, blew on it and it was alive. A while after this the community's cook died and Mungo's companions said he ought to be able to bring the cook back to life as he had already done so with the robin – either that or he would have to be cook. Mungo restored the cook to life. From then on St Serf was aware of the boy's abilities and began to love him deeply.

When at last Mungo decided it was time to strike out on his own St Serf was displeased and tried to stop him. Eventually the younger man managed to cross the Forth and when he saw his mentor approaching a boat on the other side of the river, he summoned up a storm to prevent St Serf crossing after him. After this Mungo met an old pagan who said he had foreseen that he would meet a great saint and be converted to Christianity before dying. So Mungo baptised the old man and he promptly died. Mungo put the body on a cart drawn by oxen and decided that he would found his first church where the beasts stopped. This they eventually did by the Molendinar burn. He built a simple wooden structure on the site of what is now Glasgow Cathedral.

For a while Mungo was forced to go and live in Wales. The story goes that he chose the site of his church there by following a wild boar. The boar, of course, figures strongly in the ancient legends of the Celtic-speaking peoples and is a strong pagan symbol.

In all of the stories of St Mungo he seems quite unlike what we tend to believe early missionary saints were like – he indulges in magic and weather-raising and when he has come to the court of the King of Strathclyde he actively protects an adulterous queen. Of course, early saints' Lives from all over Europe are full of magical twists and turns. Whoever or whatever Kentigern initially was, it seems at least a possibility that he is one of those figures from the far pagan past recreated in Christian times.

## St Maelruba

Opposite the Isle of Raasay (A25) on the coast of Wester Ross is the tiny village of Applecross (A31). This quaintly named settlement has nothing to do with apples. Rather, it is an old, probably Pictish name, Apur-Crossan, meaning the mouth of the Crossan, the local burn. It is associated with a saint who has been the cause of much speculation, St Maelruba. Placenames associated with him are various. Loch Maree (A32) and its island Eilean Maree, twenty-five kilometres to the northeast, are believed to be named for him. So was Amulree (D30), north of Crieff, and it is his fair that was celebrated in Banff (B22) as the Summareve Fair. In the late seventeenth century divination rites were still being carried out in the saint's name in Easter Ross as was the well-known bull sacrifice on Eilean Maree, itself also known as St Mourie's Isle. The picture is further complicated by some commentators seeing the first element of his name, mael or maol as Gaelic for cropped or bald, in reference to his tonsure perhaps. The belief is that like most of the early Gaelic monks, he cut his hair from ear to ear and let it grow long at the back – a practice thought to have originated with the druids. (The traditional Christian tonsure left a ring of hair round the entire head, of course.) Whatever the origin of the name of this complex figure, local belief in the powers associated with him lasted a long time. Even in the mid-nineteenth century lunatics were taken to St Mourie's Isle to kneel before the weatherworn altar, drink from the sacred waters of the loch and then be dipped three times in the loch itself. The beneficent powers of the well were thought to be at their peak on the saint's day, 25 August. He was long referred to as the 'God Mourie'.

## St Merchard

Another saint to whom supplications were made was St Merchard. He is believed to have been one of the first Christian missionaries to have come into the west central Highlands, although it is unclear whether he came as a follower of Columba or of the even earlier saint Ninian, said to have converted the Picts. He founded several churches in the Glenmoriston area (A30) on the west of the Great Glen. His main foundation was in Glenmoriston below the ancient hillfort of Dun Dreggan (A29) where the mighty Finn Mac Cuill was said to have slain a dragon.

On his death Merchard left instructions that his body was to be placed in an ox-cart and the oxen set moving. Wherever they stopped, that was where he was to be buried. (This is the same method used by St Kentigern to locate his church.)

Like several other saints Merchard left a bell with miraculous powers behind him, kept in the church at Clachan Merchard. The bell had the power to ring of its own accord whenever a funeral approached the kirkyard. One dark night the locals were awakened in the middle of the night by Merchard's bell. Several of them headed at once to the kirkyard, where they found the body of a freshly-murdered man. The murderer was found nearby and subjected to the justice of the time – hanging.

The bell shared another feature with other Celtic bells: it could fly back to its home if removed. Whenever it was installed in a new church it would fly back to Clachan Merchard. At last in the seventeenth century the old church collapsed beyond repair and a new one had to be built some distance away. The bell was left on a tombstone in the original kirkyard where it remained for over a century until some unfortunate stole it. Despite this, Merchard himself lingered in the area a long time.

One of the clan laws that in some areas survived very late was the each-ursain, the horse fine. This was fine which the clan chief could levy on a family which had lost one of its male members. It was derived from the old clan obligation to fight on behalf of the clan when called on to do so by the chief. In this case, however, the fine – livestock to the value of a horse – was being levied on a distraught widow, long after the warrior function of the clansmen had ceased. The chief, MacPhatrick, sent his law-officer to do the dirty work of removing almost all the sheep that the widow had, leaving her effectively destitute. The woman prayed that night to St Merchard. The same night the law-officer was awakened by a thunderous voice which declared to him: 'I am great Merchard of the miracles, passing homeward in the night. Declare thou unto MacPhatrick that the widow's sheep will never bring him good.'

The terrified law-officer fell out of bed and ran to rouse his master and tell him what had happened. The sheep were returned to the widow and MacPhatrick never again tried to turn old clan law to his own advantage. Would that other lairds had been likewise restrained.

## St Columba

St Columba is a figure of great importance in Scottish history, politically as well as religiously. He became important to Scotland partly because of something that happened in the seventh century. Columba's followers had clashed with mainstream Christian practise up until the Synod of Whitby in 664. The clashes had to do with practises in the early Gaelic church, mainly concerned with different tonsure and ways of calculating Easter. This continued even after Adomnán, abbot of Iona (A17), nominally accepted Roman practice, and thus the superiority of Rome at Whitby. (Adomnán was a kinsman of Columba and his most determined defender.) The ancient rites of the Columban Church were thus carried on for centuries in many of our leading cathedrals by those religious communities called Culdees who existed alongside the official Roman Church into the early Middle Ages. Reference to this allowed the post-Reformation Church in Scotland to claim an earlier pedigree than the now despised Catholic Church.

Columba, however, was already a major personality in his own lifetime. A member of the Uí Néill dynastic family in Ulster, he probably had a right to be a king in Ireland himself but opted instead for the religious life.

One of the best-known stories concerning Columba involves plagiarism. Columba made a secret copy of a psalter belonging to another cleric without getting the owner's permission. This was considered a serious crime and at a special ecclesiastical court he was found guilty of transgressing the law and ordered to hand over the copy to the owner of the original. Columba refused to accept the judgement. He went further and called on his kinsmen to support him. The situation worsened and eventually a battle was fought in which many men died. After this Columba was sent into exile in Scotland with the instruction to convert at least as many new souls to Christianity as he had caused to be killed in the battle. This is how he came to Iona. Many laments attributed to the saint record his sadness at leaving Ireland.

Columba was also a noted bard and he spoke on behalf of the traditional rights of bards in Irish society at the Convention of Drum Ceat in 575. The bards had originally been one of the druidic orders and Columba went so far as to call Christ his 'Druid' in one work. In another he refers to his greatest fear as the sound of an axe in 'the oak groves of Derry.' (Doire Cholmchille – the oak grove of Columba – is the full name of Derry today.)

On Iona there is a site called Reilig Orain, the burial place of Oran. This connects to the story of Columba arriving on the island and deciding that a human sacrifice was necessary to appease the spirits of the island! One of his monks, Oran, offered himself as the sacrifice and was buried alive. Three days later Columba opened up the grave and found Oran was still alive. He told Columba that death was no marvel and Hell was not as it was said to be. The saint was greatly offended at this and ordered that the grave be filled in again. This suggests either a garbled version of some kind of initiation or possibly the very old tradition of burying a human in the foundations of a new building as a form of sacrifice.

While at the Pictish court in Inverness Columba was involved in a battle of magic with the king's druid, Broichan, in which control of the weather was one of the main areas of combat. The idea of the great Christian saint taking part in a battle of magic seems a bit strange today but back in the Dark Ages, and even into medieval times, such ideas were not unusual.

## St Abban

The Isle of Jura is steeped in mythology and legend. It has its own goddess figure and a range of hills known as the Paps of Jura with three, not two, peaks. At its northern end is the great whirlpool Corryvreckan (C17), the legendary significance of which is discussed above. A goddess on Jura was said to protect her deer from any non-Jura hunters. Today its largely uninhabited northern end has vast herds of red deer. In such a location it is not surprising that the stories of early Christian figures should have suggested pagan belief patterns.

Such a one is St Abban who lived on the island with his granddaughter. One day, while out trying to catch fish, the old saint was washed off the rocks and drowned. The child somehow managed by herself and grew into a healthy young woman. One day while on the seashore collecting driftwood near where her grandfather had been swept away she inadvertently picked up a small piece of bone lying on the beach. At home she put the bone in with the kindling and later flung it with some of the driftwood onto the fire. Soon the bone was alight and a spark from it flew out and burned the girl. Nine months later St Abban was born again from the womb of his own grandchild. Here again we see the new faith dressing itself in old clothes to appeal more to the local inhabitants. A variant of this is the belief that it was dangerous for a virgin lass to touch either a bone or a dead body in case she became pregnant. It may also be an answer to why the water used to wash a corpse had to be poured over a stone securely fixed in the earth and capable of absorbing its force.

# CHAPTER 6

# Supernatural Beings

SCOTLAND IS LIKE ALL OTHER lands in that our traditions have many stories about supernatural beings, friendly and otherwise. In the Chapter 1 we saw some of the tales associated with fairies but there are many more supernatural beings. There are wondrous waterhorses called kelpies, those strange sea-creatures, the silkies, who could take human or seal form, domestic spirits like the brownies and gruagachs and the truly mysterious Nessie, who many still believe in.

## *Nessie*

Loch Ness is a fitting location for a mystery. This great body of water is over thirty kilometres long and has storms that are almost as bad as those at sea. Its origin is itself the subject of legend but for many centuries it is best known for its mythological inhabi-

Nessie

tant, Nessie. Nowadays the monster of Loch Ness (generally considered to be female) is looked on without fear or horror but in her first recorded appearance she is a truly frightening creature.

According to Adomnán's Life of Columba the saint was on his way to Inverness when he and his companions came to the banks of the River Ness. They came across a group of men burying one of their number who had been killed by a water monster in the river. Spotting a boat on the far side of the river, he sent one of his monks to swim over for the boat. Just as the monk reached midstream a great monster arose out of the river, gave a great roar and bore down on the unfortunate man. The creature was within a few feet of the monk when Columba raised his hand and commanded the monster to stop. The monster reared back in terror, turned and fled back into the waters of the river. The monk swam to the other shore and got the boat to ferry his companions across. The watching locals were mightily impressed and thereafter had a great respect for the 'God of the Christians'. Whether or not this is just another instance of a saint's miracle it is intriguing that there have never been any stories of Nessie attacking a human since!

## Kelpies

Another type of water-creature known all over Scotland is the kelpie, each uisge or water horse. Although its form was usually that of a horse, the kelpie had the ability to change its shape and often appeared as a handsome young man and occasionally as a bonnie young woman. The kelpie's intent was almost always to lure its victims into the river and drown them and this may be an idea that originated from the dangers presented in trying to cross rivers in the long years before bridges were built. Most kelpies are said to have magnificent bridles which had magic powers themselves and anyone lucky enough to find a kelpie's bridle would be able to see all the invisible beings that populate our atmosphere by looking through the eyelets of the bridle.

# Loch Slochd

One time in the not-so-distant past Seumas McGregor was on his way from Inverness to Glenlivet. He had made it as far as Loch Slochd (B25) when he had to rest. He was sitting thinking he should have made the journey on horseback when suddenly his own horse appeared in front of him, saddled, bridled and waiting to be mounted. Hardly thinking, Seumas climbed up on the horse's back and off he set eastward. They had hardly gone more than a short distance when the horse began veering towards the loch. At once Seumas realised what was happening: he had got on a kelpie's back! At once he cried out the name of the Trinity. The horse reared up and threw its rider, then dashed into the loch. Seumas was knocked out. When he awoke he found himself lying on the path with the kelpie's bridle firmly clasped in his hands. This bridle was said to be in the possession of a local man called Warlock Willie in Gaulrig, Banffshire, last century, and has since been used to help many people.

Not all who met kelpies escaped so lightly. Near the Bridge of Luib on the River Don is a boulder known locally as the Kelpie's Stane. One day a man came to the crossing point on the way to the funeral of a dead cousin. There had been torrential rain a few days earlier and the bridge had been carried away as the river flooded. Just as he was thinking of turning back a tall man appeared and said he would carry him to the other side. With the thought of his cousin's funeral bearing heavily on his mind, the traveller accepted the offer. As they reached the middle of the river the man whose shoulder he was sitting on turned into a fearsome horse. He had hitched a ride from a kelpie! Struggling furiously, the traveller managed to wrest himself from the kelpie's clutches and swim to the shore. The furious kelpie reared up and threw a massive boulder at him, which just missed him. This is the Kelpie's Stane. A similar tale is told of Shielhill Bridge near Memus (D9) in Angus and here the stone bears the mark of a kelpie's cloven hoof.

# Loch Pityoulish

A tale is told of the kelpie that inhabited Loch Pityoulish (B28) near the River Spey in the foothills of the Grampian Mountains.

A group of young lads including the heir of Kincardine were playing by the loch. Suddenly a lovely black horse with a beautiful silver harness and richly carved saddle trotted along the bank towards them. The horse came right up to the boys and bowed its head as if to ask the boys to climb on its back. Immediately some of them climbed on its back while others stroked its bridle and its mane. Suddenly young Kincardine realised his hand was stuck to the horse's mane. This was no horse, he realised, just as the creature reared up and leapt into the loch. Into the waters it crashed, dragging the young lads down to the depths. Young Kincardine was stuck fast to its mane but he knew what he had to do. As they sank ever deeper he pulled out his dirk with his free hand and without hesitation he sliced off the fingers attached to the mane. He floated free and swam to the surface trailing blood as his companions were drowned in the dark waters of the loch. He had lost the fingers of one hand, but his quick-thinking had saved his life.

# Loch nan Dubrachan

Loch nan Dubrachan in Skye is another body of water with a kelpie. One of the stories associated with it is that the kelpie there decided to live as a human for a while. Like all its kind the creature was handsome as a man, dark-haired and well-built as well. As is the way of such things, the handsome young man took the fancy of a local lass called Morag and before too long the couple were married. In the fullness of time a child was born. Morag was aware that her husband sometimes went off on his own for what she thought were long walks by the loch shore. One night, after he had been on one of these walks she looked closely at him lying sleeping beside her and started back in horror. There among the dark curled hair on his chest was sand! She knew then that this was no man, but a kelpie. Raising the bedclothes gently she slipped form the bed, dressed, wrapped her child in a blanket and fled from the house, never to return. It was said that for many years the kelpie could be heard in Loch nan Dubhrachan (A28) singing a sad song of his loneliness and wishing for the return of his Morag.

## A Female Kelpie

Near Trotternish, also on Skye, there was another legendary kelpie. A bunch of young lasses were up at the shielings on Shadowy Hill one evening looking after the cattle. When they had lain down to sleep on the big communal bed of bracken and heather, they heard a quavering voice outside the bothy door asking to be let in. They looked to see who it was, and there was a little old woman who said she had lost her way. They let her in and said she could share their bed. The frail old woman said she was frightened of sleeping at the foot of the bed or at the back of the bed. The upshot was that the lasses, feeling sorry for her, let her sleep in the middle of them. The lass sleeping nearest the door of the bothy noticed that the old woman was restless and that she seemed to sleep only in bursts. Just as she herself was drifting off, she sensed the old woman moving about and turned to look. There she saw a terrible sight: the old woman had crawled right up next to one of the girls and had fastened her teeth in her arm. Screaming, the lass watching got up and made for the door. She wrenched the door open and ran as quickly as she could. Down the hillside she ran, pursued by the kelpie. She came to a stream near the church of Bracadale (A19) and just as the cock crew in nearby Balgowan, the maiden leapt over the stream. The kelpie could not cross the stream and, seeing its prey escape moaned, 'Duilich e, duilich e, alltan,' meaning, 'Sad it is, sad it is, little streamlet'. Ever since then the burn has been known as the Alltan Duilich.

# Silkies

Kelpies are not the only shape-shifting water-creature that can assume human shape. There is also the silkie, a sea-creature half seal and half human, stories of which are known through the Outer Hebrides and the northern archipelagos of Orkney and Shetland. One of the best known of the silkies is the hero of the great Scots ballad 'The Silkie of Sule Skerrie' which is a rocky isle about forty kilometres west of Orkney. In one verse the silkie says

I am a man upon the land,
An I am a silkie in the sea,
An when I'm far an far frae land,
My hame it is in Sule Skerrie.

This ballad tells a tragic tale with its haunting tune: the silkie has a son by a human lass who goes on to marry a gunner. The silkie comes to her in a dream and foretells the gunner will kill him, which comes to pass.

This is something all of silkie tales have in common – they are always sad. Some feature men with silkie wives whom they captured by getting hold of their skins while the silkies were in human

Silkies

65

form. Such silkie-women bore them children and were good mothers and wives but their seal skins had to be kept hidden or they would slip into them and return to their home below the waves, abandoning husband and children.

The Clan MacCodrum from North Uist (A10) are said to be descended from silkies. The belief is very ancient and linked to the idea that the silkies were attendants of the King of Lochlann, a magical kingdom which, initially an Otherworld location, became identified with Norway. Perhaps the seals were the totem of the MacCodrums in times gone by, for they would never do any harm to a seal.

Once there was a man who made his living from fishing and catching seals in the north of Scotland near John o Groats (B4). One day when he was out walking he saw a massive bull seal lying on a rock ahead of him. He ducked down and crept closer. When he was a few feet from the great beast he drew out his knife and leapt out to stab the creature. Up it reared, knocking him back off his feet and in an instant it had fled into the water taking his good knife with it. He was disappointed but soon forgot all about it. A few weeks later late in the evening a dark stranger came to his door. The stranger was mounted on a black mare with grey mane and tail. He told the fisherman that his master wanted to do business with him; he should get on his horse and follow. The fisherman told him he had no horse, and the stranger offered to take him up behind him. The fisherman, intrigued by the obvious wealth of the stranger, was happy to go along and meet the man's master. At once they took off and the horse went like the wind. Soon they were standing on the cliffs overlooking the Pentland Firth. Puzzled, the fisherman asked where they were going and at that the horseman galloped forward. The three of them soared out into the air and crashed into the sea hundreds of feet below. Deeper and deeper they went but the fisherman could see everything around him and seemed to have no trouble breathing. After a while the horseman lifted his arm and pointed. There in the distance was a great white palace on the sea bed. They came near the magnificent building and all around them were seal-folk – men, women and children – all weeping. At last they were at the palace and entered through its great green doors. He was taken through many rooms until they came to a dimly lit chamber where a great seal lay stretched on a bed, moaning in pain. As the fisherman approached he saw a blood-stained knife on a small table by the bed. Looking closer he recognised his own knife. His guide then spoke and told him this was the King of the Seals, his own father, and he was dying. The horseman asked his pardon for deceiving him but he had had no alternative.

'It is I who need pardon from you for what I have done to your father,' said the fisherman.

'Lay your hand on the wound,' said his guide.

Doing so, the fisherman was amazed to see the wound heal over immediately. The great old seal rose up and thanked him.

Before they would let the fisherman go he was asked to swear that he would never hunt seals again and once he had done so he was assured that whenever he cast his nets in future he would always get a good catch. The great, grey seal bade him farewell and, mounted once again behind his guide, the fishermen was returned to his home. When he had dismounted, the Seal King's son once more thanked him and handed him a small leather bag before wheeling his horse round and disappearing at a great speed. The fishermen went in to his wife and told her all that had happened and when he opened the bag he found it full of beautiful pure-white pearls.

Not all supernatural beings are necessarily evil as the above story shows. Tradition has preserved tales of many other supernatural creatures who are actively beneficial to humankind.

## Urisks

On the northern slopes of Ben Venue (C13) overlooking Loch Katrine in the Trossachs is Coire nan Urisgean. A coire, or corry, is a bowl-shaped depression on a mountain or hill, though in some cases its meaning explicitly suggests 'cauldron'. This particular corry is said to be where all the urisks of Scotland would gather.

The urisks were said to be a race of forest-dwelling spirits with long hair, long teeth and claws and were half human, half goat. They were shy creatures, haunting the high mountain tops and deep woods of the Highlands. Initially they were believed to have been hostile to humans but over the years, like other spirits, some of them became attached to human families. The house of Tullochgorum (B29) in Strathspey had a pair of these creatures, male and female, the female being known as Mag Mulloch. She was said to be an excellent domestic servant but used to tell the mistress of the house of the misdeeds of other servants. She also had the interesting task of escorting the Laird of Tullochgorum when he was drunk. The name Mag Mulloch means 'hairy Meg', and this suggests a link to another form of spirit, the gruagach, whom we shall meet soon.

## Brownies

Brownies were known for the help they gave. They were simple-seeming creatures, seldom to be seen during the day but active after nightfall when they would perform all sorts of domestic and agricultural tasks. While the urisks were traditionally associated with forests, the brownies were as common in the Lowland areas and the Northern Isles as in the Highlands. All of them, however, were extremely touchy.

About nine kilometres northeast of Moffat in the Borders is the farm of Bodesbeck (D62). Once the farm had a brownie who, like most of his kind, was shy but very hard-working. All he need-ed to keep going was some food and a libation of milk left out for him at night. Many of the brownies had their milk poured into a hollow in a stone from which they might lap it up.

The Brownie of Bodesbeck was very good at looking after the animals about the place and the farm prospered with his help. One year, the weather had been particularly fine and a spectacular harvest had been brought in. There were great celebrations that year and the farmer, thinking that the brownie should share in the general benefits he had helped so much to create, left out a special meal of a loaf of white bread and a jug of cream. The brownie came out that evening as usual but rather than being pleased, he was offended the farmer should think he needed extra consideration for working hard. He immediately left the farm, reputedly saying

Caa, brownie, caa,
Aa the luck o Bodesbeck,
Awa tae Leithen Ha.

## Glaistigs and Gruagachs

Similar to the brownies were the glaistigs and gruagachs. The glaistig was generally associated with animals and dairying. Like the brownies, the glaistigs and the gruagachs liked milk, poured into hollows in stones. In Skye such stones were referred to as gruagach stones. These are reminiscent of the Stone Age cup-and ring-marks found all over Scotland and Ireland. On the misty Isle of Skye are standing stones which used to be known as gruagach stones to which islanders used to bring milk libations. Some see the pouring of libations as an echo of ancient religious practice.

The name gruagach seems to mean long-haired one. Some scholars have noted that the name is very like that of the grach, druidesses who lived on the Isle of Sena off the Brittany coast in ancient times. The name may be related to Welsh gwrach, meaning hag or witch. The term survived into the nineteenth century in Pembrokeshire where the last sheaf of the harvest was called gwrach, exactly as the last sheaf in Scotland was called the cailleach in Gaelic-speaking areas. A similar term for a local goddess survived in mainland Brittany into the eighteenth century. The association with the harvest and the close match of the words suggests that the names might once have been an allusion to a mother goddess.

## A Lochaber Glaistig

A story is told in Lochaber of a glaistig who was a form of water-spirit. She haunted rivers and lochs and was always ready to cause trouble. One time she set upon a horseman returning home to

The Lochaber Glaistig

Lianachan in the dead of night. This was a man known as Big Kennedy who was not one to be trifled with in any way. As she attacked him he grabbed her and, sitting her in front of him, he tied her to him with his sword belt. He headed home knowing he had been in danger of his life and that he would have to take drastic action. He kept her in his house overnight and at daybreak he heated the coulter of his plough in the kitchen fire until it was red hot. He then made the glaistig swear on the hot iron that never again would she plague the people of Lochaber while the sun shone by day or the moon by night. In doing this the glaistig burned her hand to the bone and leapt out of the window with a great shriek. She ran to a nearby hillock where she ejected three surges of blood. With each she cursed Big Kennedy and his seed forever. The hillock bore the scars ever since: where her blood poured the vegetation has been stained.

## An Argyll Glaistig

In Glen Duror (A22) there was for long time a glaistig who thought it her particular duty to prevent calves from suckling their mothers during the night.

When new tenants moved into the farm, they neglected to put out a libation for the glaistig. The following morning not a drop of milk was to be had from any cow. The situation was remedied that night and the following day things were back to normal.

Soon after this a new lass came to work on the farm. She was told to tend to the glaistig's needs, but she laughed at the very idea. That evening she went to the stream to fill a pail of water. As she knelt she got a great thump to her cheek which twisted her head half round. Try as she could, she could not move her head; it remained in a strange and twisted position. But despite all her tears nothing could be done and the next night she went to the stream again for water. As she knelt, fearful of what might happen next, she received another thump. This time it came form the other side and her head was restored to its rightful position. Here was a spirit with a mischievous sense of humour! When the farm was vacated, she stayed on and was rumoured to still be there in 1870.

# CHAPTER 7

# Witches and Warlocks

THE BEST-KENNT WITCH in Scotland is without doubt Cutty Sark from Burns's 'Tam o Shanter'. The hero is attracted to the sight of her firm young thighs and she is generally contrasted with the prevailing notion of a witch in Burns's day. What were witches meant to be like? An aged crone, an outcast possessed of so much power that people refuse her nothing? This popular notion combines nineteenth-century Gothicism and Hollywood simplicity, but it captures none of the controversy in perceptions of witches long ago.

Witch persecutions in Scotland, particularly in the aftermath of the Reformation in the late sixteenth century, were horrendous, vicious assaults. Usually 'witches' were old women rarely guilty of anything more than being friendless or utilising ancient cures that had come down through the centuries. However as the growth of masculine-dominated 'scientific' medicine began, these women were perhaps seen as an impediment to progress. In any case, Scotland's placenames are full of references to places where women were burned alive.

Various authors over the years have stressed the link between witches and a pagan religion that predated Christianity. Sacred sites often provide the link. Covens of witches are known to have gathered in kirkyards which themselves are often located on sites of pre-Christian sanctity such as at Auldearn (B17) in Moray and the Knock of Alves (B20) near Forres (B19). They also gathered on hilltops traditionally associated with the ancient fire festivals of Beltane (1 May) and Samhain (1 November) – also the main dates for the meetings of the witches themselves. These were the great feast days of the agricultural year (as discussed above) and were closely linked to fertility rites and other pagan practices. This does suggest some sort of continuity with the pagan past and it is more than likely that such cults had their own knowledge of healing as well as the more commonly stressed activities of working evil, prophesying and casting different kinds of spells.

## A Spell on Eilean Maree

The use of spells to lift disease from both man and beast survived long after the advent of Christianity in Scotland. There is little doubt that much of what the reformed Church referred to as 'popish superstition' was in fact ancient religious or healing rituals. In 1678 it is recorded that Hector Mackenzie, his son and grandson sacrificed a bull for the recovery of Christine Mackenzie who was extremely ill. This occurred on the island of St Mourie in Loch Maree, Gairloch, mentioned in connection to St Maelruba, above. It seems the cure worked but the men were called before the local presbytery and censured for this act. Twenty years later there is mention of the same kind of activity associated with St Mourie's feast day in the district of Dingwall (B12) on the opposite coast.

## Kate McNiven

To the north of the Strathearn town of Crieff (D35), long a centre of cattle trading, is the Knock of Crieff. This is an area abounding in legends. North of Knock is a standing stone, thought to be the remnant of a stone circle, known as Kate McNiven's Stane. Tradition tells that in 1583 Kate McNiven or Kate Nike Nieving was burned here. (The name Nike Nieving is clearly derived from the Gaelic Nic Nevin, meaning daughter of Nevin. In some sixteenth-century manuscripts Nike Nieving is said to be Queen of the Witches herself and there is a record of a notorious sorceress called Nic Nevin being burned in St Andrews in 1569.)

The name may also have been some sort of title, possibly within a witch cult of some kind. In Alexander Montgomerie's sixteenth-century poem 'The Flyting Betwixt Polwart and Montgomery', the name is given to the leading figure of all the

Scottish witches. The story at Crieff is that Kate had been found guilty of witchcraft at a time when the paranoia against so-called witches was at its worst. In those dark days suspicion of witchcraft alone was often enough to condemn women to a nasty and sadistic death. Some versions of the story say she was burned on the Knock of Crieff itself just above the cliff face named after her, and others that she was burned below the cave in the north face of the Knock, now known as Kate McNiven's Cave. It is there that the unfortunate woman is said to have hidden from her pursuers until she was discovered. Wherever it may have happened, when she was captured she was tied up and surrounded by faggots. Just as the torch was lit a local laird, Graham of Inchbraikie, came by and tried to put an end to the proceedings. (This was despite his being one of the original complainants against her!) His protests, however, were in vain – the representatives of the kirk (and probably the gathered crowds as well) insisted the burning went ahead. Kate had noticed Inchbraikie's attempts, though, and just as the fire caught she bit a blue bead from her necklace and spat it at him shouting that as long as he and his family kept it his house would flourish. The flames soon consumed the unfortunate woman. The blue bead she spat at Inchbraikie became a valued heirloom and the family prospered through the years. The story was repeated time and again, for thousands of folk had come from miles around to see the end of Kate McNiven.

Kate McNiven

## North Berwick Witches

One of the most striking landmarks in the Firth of Forth is the conically-shaped North Berwick Law. As I have already noted, the term 'law' often suggests a sacred site and it seems likely that North Berwick Law was suitable for the great seasonal fire festivals of Beltane and Samhain. It was here that one of the most famous witch covens in Scottish history used to meet.

In 1590, according to contemporary records, a local coven met with black work to do. A plot had been hatched by the Earl of Bothwell to murder his cousin, King James VI, and take over the throne. He was widely believed to have been initiated into the Devil's service and called upon the North Berwick coven to help implement his desires. One dark night in the port of Leith the witches gathered for a strange ceremony. They took a cat and tied gobbets of a hanged man's flesh to its paws. Incantations were muttered and then suddenly the screeching animal was flung into the seething waters of the Forth. A squall arose and a boat did founder, but it was the wrong boat. The intended victim of this bizarre ceremony was the king sailing back from Denmark with his new bride, Anne. The weather did worsen but the royal ship reached port safely.

The plot came to light when a local bailiff in Tranent, one David Seaton, began to suspect his servant Gillies Duncan was up to no good. When questioned she said nothing, but in those evil times suspicion of witchcraft was excuse enough to instigate

North Berwick witches

extreme physical brutality with the avowed intention of extracting a confession. After various sadistic actions were carried out against her, including the mangling of her hands with pilnie-winks, or thumbscrews, she cracked and began to pour out a garbled series of confessions. According to her she was part of a coven that included a young local schoolmaster, John Fian, the aristocrat Euphemia MacLean, a midwife called Agnes Sampson and a local housewife, Barbara Napier. Sampson in particular was locally well known for her herbal cures and simples. When Fian was subjected to the grisly ritual of the boot, in which the victim's feet were slowly mangled, he confessed to devil worship but later retracted his confession. Despite further torture he remained steadfast but was eventually strangled and burned on Edinburgh's Castle Hill. Sampson detailed various plots against the king including trying to get a piece of his personal clothing which she intended smearing with toad's venom. This she said would have caused him to die in torment. Tales were told of Sabbats attended by the Devil and the use of a corp creagh, or clay figure, representing the king. Napier said seven score witches were involved, while her co-accused Sampson claimed even more – 200. They described various rituals including a ring dance (once a standard at Beltane and other feasts) and a black mass. The king himself attended the trial and eventually interjected, calling all of the witches liars and effectively saying it was all fantasy.

Then came the strangest event of all. Agnes Sampson asked if she could speak to the king and tell him something only he could know. Moving off to the side, the midwife whispered something in the king's ear – the words that he had said to his new queen on their wedding night in Oslo when they were alone. This proof of supernatural powers was enough for the king and Samson and Euphemia MacLean were executed soon after. Why Sampson should want to condemn herself by convincing the king of her supernatural powers is unclear but it is more than likely she was somewhat confused, having been tortured and interrogated for a considerable time. But she did convince the king. The rest of the confessions are full of the regularly recurring ideas that crop up throughout the period – and probably correspond much more closely to the fantasies of the ministers and other interrogators than to any actual rites and activities on the part of the women.

Boswell, said to have been the originator of the foul plot, has been suggested as the 'Devil' who led the activities at the various gatherings. He fled the country, dying in Italy thirty years later supposedly having carried on his necromantic activities there.

The king became even more interested in witchcraft and in fact went on to write a book on it himself called Dæmonologie. It is likely that it was this ongoing interest which inspired William Shakespeare to include the witch scene in Macbeth, performed before the king, who was by then also James 1 of England. To this day that is probably the most famous representation of Scottish witches and one which has set the pattern for so many others since.

## The Witches of Auldearn

Just inland from the Moray coast and a few kilometres east of Nairn is Loch Loy (B18). It was here on a small farm that one of Scotland's most famous witches was raised. This was Isobel Goudie, one of the coven of witches who regularly met at the Auld Kirk of Auldearn (B67), built on the site of an earlier pagan sanctuary. This young woman was described as being very attractive with flaming red hair and mysterious dark eyes. It seems she met with a scholar of some sort in the nearby ruined Castle of Inshoch between Loch Loy (B18) and Auldearn and it was he who initiated her into the practice of witchcraft. Then she was baptised into the cult in the kirk of Auldearn itself. Later it is told that she went into the Downie Hills and met and drank with the Queen of the Fairies. She described the Devil manufacturing elf-arrow heads with his bare hands and handing over gold that turned to horse-dung within a day. She herself was shown how to make the corp creagh, or wax dummy, how to manufacture moon-paste and how to use fairy arrows. Here she also met notable people including Robert Gordon of Gordonstoun who was a privy councillor of Charles I. He was believed to have studied the black arts in Padua and Salamanca and was at last taken by the Devil near Birnie Kirk close to Elgin.

Isobel rose to some prominence in the cult but ultimately wearied of the life, gave herself up and confessed. She was tried in the very church in which she had been baptised as a witch – Auldearn – and was sentenced to be strangled and burned.

The link to the far past here is more than just the use of a sacred site. The elf-arrows Isobel Goudie talked of were long believed to be missiles from the 'little people' which were used to injure cattle or even humans. What they were is Stone Age flint arrowheads, often of remarkable workmanship. Coming across these in ploughed fields or on hillsides, people were impressed and it is little wonder that in those days before archaeology people saw such beautiful artefacts as magical rather than just remnants from the far distant past.

# The Witch of Laggan

Just north of Kingussie (B35) at the very foot of the Monadhliath Mountains there was a green mound at Laggan (B37) where a witch used to dwell. She was often known to roam through the hills above Kingussie whatever the weather, going about her evil business. One day a hunter from nearby Gaick (B39) found himself caught in a vicious storm and took shelter in a rough bothy high in the hills. With him he had two hunting hounds which were his pride and joy. He had got a fire roaring and was sitting warming himself when he heard a mewling at the door. When he opened the door, there was a bedraggled black cat. The cat said she was in fact a poor witch in need of shelter and that she deeply regretted her misdeeds and wanted to repent, if only she would let him in by the fire. The two hounds growled deep in their throats and it was clear if the cat came in they might go for it. Despite his hatred of witchcraft, the hunter felt sorry for the creature and when she suggested he tie his hounds to the rantree of the bothy with a long hair she offered him, he said he would. However, he was a man of canny disposition and shushing his well-trained dogs, he only pretended to tie them up as he fastened the hair from the rantree to another spar in the roof.

The cat then came into the fire and at once began to swell in size. Suddenly she changed into human form and the hunter recognised the notorious witch, the 'good wife of Laggan'. She let out a cackle and said that now she had him. She called out 'Fasten, hair, fasten!' The magic hair at once contracted but all that happened was that the spar in the roof broke. The two hounds fell on the witch and began rolling about the floor with her. They were eventually thrown off, leaving their teeth in the hide of the foul creature. At once the witch changed shape again, this time into a raven. She flew out of the bothy door. The two hounds had been poisoned by biting the witch and the hunter could do nothing but watch them die. He buried the faithful beasts and then, as the storm had eased a bit he returned to Gaick. Getting home he was told that the 'good wife of Laggan' had caught a chill carrying peats and lay at death's door. At once he ran to Laggan and burst into the witch's house where in front of her neighbours he pulled the bedclothes off the old hag and showed the marks of his hounds' teeth in her skin. She had been sorely wounded by the hounds and began to cry in terror for she knew that when she died, her black master, Satan himself, would come to carry her off to Hell. With a final shriek of terror the old witch died in front of the astonished gathering.

Later that night two travellers were crossing the Monadhliath mountains on their way to Speyside when they saw a terrible apparition. A screaming blood-spattered woman was fleeing across the moor towards the kirkyard of Dalarossie (B38) closely pursued by two great black hounds and a black-clad horseman. They stopped and as the horseman passed them he jocularly asked if they thought the hounds would be able to catch up on their prey before she reached the kirkyard. With a terrifying laugh he then spurred his horse and went haring off after the woman and the hounds. The men got out as fast as they could but as they came down through the woods above Kingussie the black horseman passed them again. Over his saddle bow was the woman, the hounds still clinging to her. It seems the Evil One had had his sport and taken the soul of the Witch of Laggan.

Sometimes historical figures become the focus of stories of the supernatural. It as if the stories themselves have a life that sometimes must be renewed so they can fulfil their function. While most of these are female, folklore also records a few notable warlocks.

## Michael Scot

Michael Scot was a twelfth-century mathematician and astrologer who had a reputation as a wizard throughout Europe. He travelled widely through the courts of Europe and owned a magic book which was buried with him in Melrose Abbey.

A tale is told of him catching and cooking a great white serpent near Drummochter (D1), the high pass through the Highlands south of Newtonmore (B36). It was said that the cooking of this beast gave him magic powers, as in the stories about Finn Mac

Michael Scot

Cuill and the magic salmon or the Welsh Taliesin and the Cauldron of Cerridwen, where the heroes attain special powers by sucking on their fingers burned by the cooking food. Like Thomas the Rhymer in later centuries. Scot's name became a byword all across Scotland although it was for magic and witchcraft rather than knowledge and wisdom.

## The Wizard Laird of Skene

About ten kilometres to the west of Aberdeen is the House of Skene. In the late seventeenth century Alexander Laird of Skene was thought to be one of the foremost practitioners of 'the black art'. It is said that even on the brightest day he never cast a shadow. Like Michael Scot so many years before, he travelled Europe and indulged in all sorts of necromantic practices. In Italy he barely escaped with his life when the Devil came to claim his due from a group of necromancers. Skene escaped by telling him that there was yet another man behind him – so the Devil stole his shadow. This was not the only time he kept out of Auld Clootie's clutches

The Wizard Laird was never seen without his familiars: a crow, a hawk, a magpie and a jackdaw. They were regularly seen with their master as he travelled in a coach drawn by coal-black horses with no visible harness, often on their way to the local kirk-yard. Here he was said to open up graves and lift out the bodies of unbaptised infants as food for his familiars. Often this grisly crew would wander the hills and glens of the area searching for particular herbs to be used in potions and spells. Some of these he used to dispose of witches in the surrounding district for he was a man who would brook no competition. He was a terror to the whole district.

One Hogmanay night he was late getting home and decided to use his magic coach to cross Loch Skene (B48). That cold night the loch was covered by a thin film of ice which would clearly not support any normal coach. He told his birds that he would cross the loch safely as long as they did not doubt him. Then he told his coachman to press straight ahead with the horses at a gallop and no matter what not to look back. He was told to keep his eyes straight ahead on the Hill of Fare. The coach flew out over the ice with the four birds flying close to the horses' heads. But despite his warning the coachman felt himself being forced to turn around. No matter how hard he tried, it seemed irresistible to look over his shoulder. When he did his heart leaped in his mouth. There, beside his smiling master was the Deil himself.

Behind the coach galloped two great black hounds. Just at that point the ice split behind the coach and the hounds fell into the water. The horses galloped even faster and within minutes the terrified horseman was at the door of Skene Castle. Turning to look behind him, terrified of what he would see, he was amazed to see the Laird sitting there smiling as if nothing had happened.

## An Edinburgh Warlock

The persecution of witches was widespread and long-lived and it was not always women who were the targets of the hysterical public reaction. In the middle of the seventeenth century one of Edinburgh's more notable citizens was Major Thomas Weir, commander of the City Guard and a noted Presbyterian.

He never married and his housekeeper was his spinster sister, Grizel. They appeared to be the absolute model of respectability except inasmuch as Grizel was subject to fits of extreme melancholia. Weir always did his best to help her in these situations and he was also known to be ready to pray beside the bed of anyone suffering from extreme illness or infirmity. It gradually became the subject of gossip that his capacity to pray seemed to be increased when he had his walking stick with him and that without it he hardly seemed the same man. This stick was oddly shaped and considered very unusual. Suspicions grew and Major Weir was called before the city magistrates to be interviewed. At once he confessed to a series of crimes and profligacies which shocked the city to the core. These crimes involved all sorts of wickedness and hypocrisy including incest with his sister. When she was questioned she admitted that she had been in communication with the Queen of the Fairies and not only confirmed her brother's confession but expanded on it. She claimed they could fly considerable distances and that they received all sorts of information about far-off events by magical means. The confessions could only have one outcome and they were both condemned to be strangled and then burned – which was considered a humanitarian option at the time.

The Major died first and went to his maker with a surly and impenitent air while Grizel had to be restrained from flinging off her clothes, an attempt that merely brought forward her strangulation. The Major's notorious stick was also burned and was said to have taken a long time to burn, twisting violently in the flames.

Most modern commentators are of the opinion that both the major and his sister were in fact probably suffering from some kind of delusional insanity but in those dangerous times when suspicion could be enough to bring death by burning, confessions were a guarantee of execution.

These types of confessions were obviously the result of torture and driven by deep-seated but ludicrous beliefs on the part of the inquisitors.

# CHAPTER 8

# Picts

BACK IN THE SEVENTEETH and eighteenth centuries 'Pictish' was used as a kind of general term to refer to Scottish ancestors. Constructions as far apart as Stone Age barrows and medieval deer dykes were all called Pictish. Today, some still think that anything old is Pictish, but scholars tend to put the 'Pictish Period' between 80 and 850 AD. 80 AD was the date of the battle of Mons Graupius when the Romans battled the Caledonians, later called Picts. Only the Romans have left us a record of this battle and argument still rages as to where it was fought. Not surprisingly, the Roman victory is reported as being total. The fact that the Romans retreated from Scotland north of the Forth soon after and only ever came back on temporary raids suggests a different interpretation, however.

In the middle of the ninth century the Picts amalgamated with the Scots of Dalriada – they had had several joint monarchs before this – and the country became known in time as Scotland. The Pictish language, which may have been something like Welsh, disappeared and this has led many people to speculate on the disappearance of the Picts themselves. While this has added to their mystique, the Picts are no less our ancestors than the Gaels, the Norse or the Angles.

Legends concerning the Picts are many. In one story from Fife, the Pechs (or Peghts, as they were generally called in the oral tradition) were wee short folk with red hair, long arms, broad feet and tremendous strength. They were the builders of all the old castles and forts in the land and would stand in a line from the quarry to the building site passing the stones from hand to hand until the building was finished. One version of the story says their feet were so broad that when it rained they could stand on their hands and use their feet as umbrellas!

Although the Picts left few written records and their domestic and military architecture blends in with that of other tribal peoples of Scotland, they have left one unique set of artefacts. These are the Pictish symbol stones, scattered from Fife to Farr in Sutherland and from the Western Isles to Buchan, and beyond into the Northern Isles. These beautiful stones, whose art may have influenced such works as the Books of Kells and Durrow, feature life-like animals and intricate geometric shapes that tell of a great artistic tradition. The symbol stones have become the subject of legend as much as have the Picts themselves.

## The Maiden Stone

Nestled in the shade of Bennachie (B44) in Aberdeenshire is the Maiden Stone (B43). This magnificent granite stone is fading under the onslaught of twentieth-century pollution, but the symbols can still be discerned. And its story is still vivid.

There was a young lass called the Maid of Drumdorno who was known far and wide for her beauty. She had been wooed by many local lads and had at last agreed to marry one of her suitors. The afternoon before the wedding she was alone in the farmhouse baking bannocks and cakes for the following day and all the while day-dreaming about her wedding. Suddenly she became aware that she was being watched. She looked up and there at the open window was a tall, dark and good-looking stranger. She gave a little cry. The stranger spoke and told her she was doing her work well and looked good with it but maybe she was just a bit slow. She retorted that she was as quick as anyone else but, flattered by the attentions of the handsome stranger exchanged a few words with him. She was quite clear about letting him know she was getting married the next day. He just laughed and said that was all very well but she would have to be a bit quicker at the baking to make a good wife. She took objection to this and told him so. Again he laughed and said he bet that he could build a road to the very top of Bennachie before she could finish her baking. He added that if she took the bet and he won, she would have to marry him instead of her intended. This was such a silly bet that she jokingly agreed and told the stranger to be on his way. Tipping his hat to her with a smile, he moved off.

She returned to her labours and soon all thought off the stranger had flown from her head. But a few hours later, just as the daylight was beginning to fade and the last batch of bannocks was ready to bake, she looked out the window. There in the fading light she could clearly see a brand new road leading all the way to the very top of Bennachie. She gasped and at that moment the stranger came into view. She now realised that she had entered a pact with the Devil. Panicking, she ran from the farm towards the Pittodrie woods. No one was about. She struggled to say a prayer but no words would come. The footsteps got louder and still she could not say the Lord's name. Just as the fiend caught up with her and grasped her waist, the prayer she had been unable to utter was answered, after a fashion. Instead of clutching a warm and vibrant lass the Devil was holding a piece of stone. He had been thwarted in his desires at the very last minute.

Although the lass had lost her life by being turned into stone she had been spared the fires of Hell and a great deal more besides. The abstract symbols on the stone – which has a small piece missing at the side of it where the Devil held on too hard – were said to represent the baking implements of the Maid of Drumdorno.

This tale ties together a Pictish symbol stone with the earlier causeway on Bennachie and was probably inspired by an attempt to decipher the meanings of the Pictish carvings.

## Martin's Stane

Another Pictish symbol stone whose carvings might have inspired a local story is Martin's Stane (D15) on the back road from Dundee to the village of Tealing. Like many other such stones it has a serpent and 'Z-rod' carved on it as well as a mounted figure and a Pictish beast. These truly enigmatic figures look a little like a dolphin and are frequently seen on the symbol stones. The local tale has survived in a short poem which tells of a great dragon.

Martin's Stane

It was tempit at Pittempton,
Draggelt at Badragon,
Stricken at Strikemartin,
An killt at Martin's Stane.

There was once a farmer who lived at Pittempton (D16), on the northern edge of Dundee. Now the farmer at Pittempton had been blessed by having nine daughters, all of whom he loved dearly. The eldest had recently become betrothed to a local man called Martin. One hot summer's day he was working hard in his fields. He grew thirsty and called for his eldest daughter to go to the well and fetch him a drink of water. Off she went and when after a few minutes there was no sign of her coming with the water, he sent his next eldest daughter to hurry her up. When the second daughter also did not return, he called for his third eldest daughter to go and see what was happening. And again she did not return. So one by one the farmer sent his lovely daughters to the well. When even the youngest had not returned he was sure they were playing a trick on him and went to the well himself.

There he saw a terrible sight. Round the well lay a great, coiled, dragon-like serpent. Scattered about were the limbs of his nine daughters. The beast had killed them all. He let out a great shriek and ran to summon his neighbours. Several had heard his cries and in minutes a large crowd of men and women carrying various arm implements as weapons descended on the well. Seeing them coming the dragon shot off towards the north hotly pursued by Martin who had picked up a large club. As the great scaly creature got to the Dighty Burn, Martin caught up with it and raised his club. The pursuing crowd yelled out as one, 'Strike, Martin!' and he gave the beast a crashing blow. This only served to make it double its speed and it soon outstripped him. Help was at hand, however, for horses had been brought and soon Martin and several others were in hot pursuit of the monster. Soon they had it surrounded and after a short struggle killed and buried the fearsome beast. It is on this spot that tradition tells that Martin's Stane was raised and the village of Strathmartin itself, close to Pittempton is said to have once been called Strikemartin.

## A Pictish Centre?

Other Pictish stones were once to be found in this area, one with a carving of a man with a large club over his shoulder. Others, of which one is in nearby Dundee Museum, all had serpents of different kinds on them. This suggests some sort of important Pictish centre here, perhaps a temple of some sort. What is certain, however, is that this is not the only story of the nine maidens. The hills to the north of the stone have a different nine maidens who were known as Pictish saints, and other tales tell of similar events in Aberdeenshire where there are Nine Maidens wells in many locations. There are also links to King Arthur and the nine maidens of Avalon, Apollo and the nine muses and the Norse god Heimdall who had nine mothers. Perhaps what we have here is a remnant of a memory of groups of pagan priestesses. Whatever the Nine Maidens were, their hold on the public imagination lasted a long time.

## Sueno's Stone

There is a strong connection with Scandinavia in the story of Sueno's Stone. Though the stone itself was found buried in the eighteenth century, the tale carries us back to the Dark Ages. We are told that the stone commemorates a battle between the local people and an invading force of Norsemen. Fighting had been going on for many years as the Norsemen had started to settle in the area. In the struggle for overall control of Moray the principal antagonists were Maelbrigde, the Mormaor of Moray and the Norse Jarl Sigurd. (Mormaor and Jarl are terms meaning something close to 'high chief'.) They agreed to settle matters once and for all by a battle where each would bring forty horsemen. On the chosen day Maelbrigde, known as 'the Buck-toothed' because of a peculiarly long eyetooth he had like an animal's fang, set off for the battlefield. As they approached the selected spot they saw the forty Norse horses ahead. However, each of the Norsemen's horses carried two warriors – Maelbrigde had been tricked. With such an advantage the Norsemen were assured of victory and the men of Moray were all killed. In celebration of this victory the Norse beheaded their enemies and returned to their camp, each astride a horse. Sigurd, in emulation perhaps of ancient tribal tradition, had taken Maelbrigde's head with him and slung it from the pommel of his saddle. As they rode, singing of their triumph, and no doubt drinking in celebration, Maelbrigde's bucktooth began rubbing on Sigurd's thigh, eventually piercing the skin. Although superficially just a scratch, the wound festered and within three days Sigurd died in agony from blood-poisoning. Maelbrigde had his revenge.

## Vanora's Stone

Another Pictish symbol stone with a remarkable story can be found in the wonderful little museum of Pictish symbol stones in the Strathmore village of Meigle (D14), twenty kilometres northwest of Perth. Among this collection is the great cross-slab known to locals as Vanora's Stone. Vanora's Stone is unusual in that it once formed part of a complex linked monument of different stones although we have

Vanora's Stone

no clear idea of how it used to look. On the side opposite the magnificent cross there is a scene which has been interpreted by various learned commentators as representing Daniel in the lion's den. It shows a gowned figure flanked by four-legged animals with heavy shoulders or manes. (Many Pictish symbol stones show both biblical and pagan iconography and in pre-literate societies it is feasible that older stories could be attached to biblical symbolism.)

The legend of Vanora's Stone involves King Arthur. There are many places in Scotland that bear the name of Arthur – Arthur's Seat in Edinburgh, Ben Arthur (C14) in Cowal, another Arthur's Seat (D11) further up Strathmore from Meigle, and a handful of them are scattered in the landscape around Meigle. The mythical Arthur was almost certainly common amongst the traditions of all the P-Celtic-speaking tribal peoples of Britain (whose languages survive as Welsh, Cornish and Breton). The idea of Arthur belonging as much to Pictish Scotland as to Wales or Cornwall is not really strange at all, even though the Pictish language itself died out over a thousand years ago.

Vanora was the wife of the great king, Arthur. Having defeated his enemies, Arthur decided to go on a pilgrimage to Rome, leaving his nephew Mordred as regent. Hardly had he set out when Vanora became involved with Mordred and they began to rule the land together. Whether Vanora was seduced by Mordred or the other way around is unclear but they soon ruled as man and wife with the support of Mordred's own Pictish troops. Arthur was still in Britain when he heard the news and immediately headed north to raise his followers and remove the usurpers. The battle where Mordred and Arthur are said to have met was at Camlaan, on the Forth, itself the site of a sixth-century battle. Mordred was defeated and killed, but Arthur was also fatally wounded and soon passed away. Vanora was imprisoned on the great Iron Age fort on nearby Barry Hill (D20) while her fate was decided. She was guilty of adultery but had betrayed the king and, therefore, his people. Such was the blackness of her deeds, the story goes, that the wisemen and priests who considered her fate decided she should be made to suffer as dishonourable a death as possible. So it was decided she should be ripped apart by a pack of wild dogs. The sentence was duly carried out. And this is the how the locals interpreted the scene on the cross-slab.

Following her execution, her body was buried as oaths and imprecations were heaped upon her burial in a manner very suggestive of ancient pagan practice. This burial is said to be in Vanora's Mound in the kirkyard of Meigle and it was believed until recently that any young woman foolish enough to stand upon Vanora's Mound would be made barren – such was the power of the curses heaped upon it so long ago. This was clearly not known to a local photographer who until quite recently had the habit of posing happy newly-weds on the mound!

## Norrie's Law

A mile or so north of Largo Law (D51) on the north side of the Forth is a hill said to have received its cleft shape from a ploughshare thrown by the Devil. In the same place on the farm of Auchendowie there used to be a tumulus, or burial mound. The site of the mound is still marked on maps though little now remains of what was known locally as Norrie's Law (D49). On the slopes of Largo Law itself until a generation or two back children would play a widely-known game with a particular local variant. One child would stand in front of a group of pals and say,

'A'll tell ye a story aboot Tammie o Norrie if ye dinnae speak in the middle o it. Will ye no?'

The intention is to make one of the other, probably younger children say no and thus prevent the story from being told. The difference from most versions of this bairns' game is the mention of Tammie o Norrie, an unfortunate local cowherd.

It was told that a ghost haunted the slopes of Largo Law, condemned to roam the earth until he could unburden himself of the secret he had died to save: the location of buried gold on Largo Law. A local shepherd on Balmain (D50) farm became obsessed with the idea of this gold and decided that he would approach the ghost and relieve it of its burden. It took all his courage but one evening he went to Largo Law as night fell, hoping to meet the unfortunate spirit. He soon spotted the ephemeral figure and approached him, asking what was keeping it from its rest. The spectre looked long at him and the shepherd's blood ran cold. Then the spirit spoke:

If Auchendowrie cock disnae craw
An the herd o Balmain disnae blaw,
A'll tell ye where the gowd is on Largo Law.

This was to have been at eight o'clock the following evening. The shepherd, excited at the notion of impending riches, did his best to ensure the ghost's conditions would be met. That night the rooster of Auchendowrie farm mysteriously disappeared. The shepherd went the following morning to speak to the cowherd of Balmain, Tammie O Norrie. After trying to wheedle him into not blowing his horn to summon the cattle into the byre that evening, he finally threatened to kill him if he dared do so. Sure that he had frightened Tammie sufficiently, the shepherd made his way to Largo Law as eight o'clock approached. Just as the wraith appeared and was about to speak, the sound of a cow horn floated through the air from Balmain. The ghost, deprived of its release from earthly torment, spat forth the words

Woe tae the man that blew that horn,
Fae oot o that spot he shall neer be borne

... and disappeared.

In a blind rage the shepherd ran north, the thought of killing the Balmain cowherd pulsing in his mind. When he got to what is now the site of Norrie's Law he was too late. There stood the figure of Tammie o Norrie, horn at his lips, having been turned to stone. The local people tried to shift the unfortunate man, but a magical force prevented them. Instead, they heaped a great mound of earth over the cowherd and this was given the name of Norrie's Law.

This story seems to be a degenerate version of an even older tale. In this rendition, the mound contains the body of a warrior called Norroway who was buried astride his horse in a suit of silver armour. What we do know is that in the 1830s a local cadger, or carter, was digging sand out of the hill when he made a remarkable discovery of silver. Over a few years he sold most of it to a silversmith in Cupar (D47) who melted it down and re-used it. Eventually the cadger's conscience got the better of him and he handed over the few remnants he had to the widow of the local landowner, the recently deceased General Durham. She in turn donated the material to the then Museum of Antiquities and the few magnificent remnants of the original Norrie's Law hoard can be seen in the new Museum of Scotland. These are a few bits and pieces including a pair of pins with Pictish symbols, a couple of lozenge-shaped items that might once have been part of a corselet of mail and pieces of a sword hilt, helmet and scabbard.

## The Sleeping Pict

Robert Louis Stevenson wrote about the Picts in his poem 'The King of the Picts', but his father had a closer connection to that ancient people. He was in Orkney surveying a site for a new lighthouse when he and a colleague were visited in their lodgings by a distraught local. He begged them to come with him and help him and his neighbours with a desperate problem. Their help was sought because they were educated men and whatever the problem was it was clearly taxing the powers of the local community.

He told them that a Pict had turned up in their village. This was met with utter disbelief by Stevenson and his friend but the local was insistent. He described a wee dark, hairy man with great big feet, clad in strangely shaped shoes, dressed in rags and without speech. He had come into the village and collapsed. The engineers were hardly keen to go outside – it was a wild night and they were comfortable by the fire. However the man was in such a state of distress that they thought they should try and help. At last they agreed to go.

When they reached the nearby village they were ushered into a humble cottage, surrounded by a crowd, even in the biting cold. Inside, yet more people were grouped around a bed on which lay the Pict. The mood of the people was sombre, and mutterings of 'Get rid of it' could be heard. In truth, the man asleep on the bed was very small, not much over four feet, and had a mass of unkempt hair and a big black beard. His clothes were made of rags stitched together and his feet were encased in extremely crude boots, obviously hand-made by someone with little if any cobbling skill.

Stevenson recognised the sleeping Pict. He was a man who had been a shopkeeper in Edinburgh until one day he got the call to go on the road and spread the word of the Lord. He gave away all his worldly goods and left the city to wander wherever his feet took him, spreading the Gospel and living as simply as he could. He had eventually ended up in Orkney, got lost, and by the time he found the village he was in a state of absolute exhaustion, made worse by not having eaten for several days, if not longer. His life on the road accounted for his appearance and he had naturally made his own boots, with no skill or instruction in that particular art. The villagers took some convincing but when the Pict at last opened his eyes, recognised Stevenson and spoke to him in Scots, their scepticism disappeared. They feared no more that an ancient Pict had burst forth from a burial mound to wreak havoc among them.

# CHAPTER 9

# Giant Lore

ALL OVER SCOTLAND SCRAPS of ancient mythology survive about giants. In Cromarty it is said that two vast boulders lying on the beach near Edderton (B9) were flung from the Hill of Struie, locally called Gilltrax. A variant of the same story concerns the Goors of Gowrie (D19), flung by the Devil from St Andrew's (D48) to Invergowrie, just west of Dundee. Another tale tells of a Deil's Stane flung by the giant on Norman's Law (D46) at the giant who resided on Dundee Law. In fact such tales are commonly used to explain the rocky slopes of many Scottish and Irish hills and mountains. Another famous giant the hill of Bennachie (B44) in Aberdeenshire, famous in story and song and the site of many ancient monuments. An ancient ballad tells us the story.

## Lang Johnnie Moir

Lang Johnnie Moir hailed from Rhynie, the village at the foot of Bennachie. At twenty years of age he was over four metres tall and was a full two metres across the shoulder. Even Johnnie's sword was three metres long. He was of an adventurous disposition and one day he headed off to London without letting anyone know. A giant like him was sure to catch the eye and he was not long in the English capital when a bonnie young lass fell in love with him. The feeling was entirely mutual but there was a problem. The lass Johnnie had fallen for was none other than the King of England's daughter. When the king heard of what was happening he locked the young lass up in a tower and left her there to starve. He would not hear of a daughter of his going to marry a Scottish common-er, even if he was a giant. There and then he sent out men to appre-hend the young giant whom he intended to hang from a tall, tall tree. On hearing this Johnnie said the king was welcome to try and

Lang Johnnie Moir

capture him. However, kings are never loath to use cunning instead of courage and men were dispatched to spike Johnnie's nightly gallon of ale.

When Johnnie awoke he found himself bound in thick iron bands and chains. Luckily, he had made friends with a wee lad who worked in his lodgings and the young lad agreed to go all the way to Rhynie for help. Off went the lad over brae and burn, by hill and river. Arriving in Rhynie he went immediately to the tallest giant he could find there. This was Auld Johnnie, the young giant's uncle, and the wee lad told him to get to London quick and to bring Jock o Noth with him. Jock o Noth was the giant who lived on the Tap o Noth (B40) another dominating hill some twenty kilometres west of Bennachie. Auld Johnnie ran up to Mither Tap on Bennachie and called out to Jock o Noth to come and help rescue young Johnnie. Even that distance away Jock heard the call and in no time at all the two great giants were on their way south to London. What a sight they made as they hurried south, looming above the trees, their brows a metre across and their shoulders near three metres broad.

When they got to London they found the gates of the City locked and barred against them and from inside they could hear the sound of a slow drum beat and the ringing of church bells.

Auld Johnnie hammered on the gate and demanded to know

what was going on from the gatekeeper who looked out of a window at the knocking. The gatekeeper said it was nothing much, they were just about to hang a great big Scot called Lang Johnnie Moir.

At this the giants demanded entry and finally kicked a great hole in the city walls and clambered through. They hastened to the town hall and there they saw the young giant on the gibbet tree, a noose around his neck.

Before anything else was done the great giant asked his nephew what he had been charged with that these Londoners meant to hang him. When they heard that the sentence was for falling in love, the two giants were furious and their rage grew even more when they heard how Johnnie had been captured. Drawing their swords, they demanded that the shackles and bands be removed and Johnnie be returned his good broadsword. Despite being brave and battle-hardened men, the King's guard had no intention of trying to fight with these gigantic warriors, now brandishing their massive broadswords over their heads. Johnnie was released.

They wasted no time heading directly to the king's palace, demanding to see his daughter. The terrified king sent for his daughter to be released and brought to the palace. Then a priest was summoned and the young couple were wed. The giants spurned the offer of a dower from the king – they were all as rich as they needed to be with castles and farms, plenty of men to work the land, flocks and herd beyond number and countless chests brimming with gold. Then there was one of the finest wedding celebrations ever seen in old London town, lasting all of seven days and seven nights, although the king did not appear to enjoy it much. Then the newly-weds headed back to Bennachie with the two old giants and the wee lad who had carried the message.

## The Fianna

Scotland has many tales of Finn Mac Cuill and the Fianna, or Fenians, a legendary warrior-band whose origins are in early Irish literature. In later tradition, they are known as a race of ancient giants, stories of which entranced generations of Gaelic speakers

at ceilidhs throughout much of Scotland. The Fianna's presence is
marked in placenames and legends throughout Scotland. The basis
for the stories seems to have been a practice in ancient Irish and
Scottish tribal society where young men would gather together in
bands during the summer to learn and practice military skills and
hunting. This was how individual lads became tribal warriors and
these groups could also be used to defend the land against
invaders and slave-raiders. In some cases they would even hire
themselves out as mercenaries. And it kept the young men out
from under the feet of everyone else.

The Sma Glen (D31) is an area rich in traditions of the Fianna.
At Fendoch (D32), overlooking the A822 north of Crieff, there is
said to have been a wooden palisaded fort inhabited in the distant
past by the Fianna. They lived here with their wives, also of gigantic stature. One day Finn and his companions decided to go and
hunt for wild boar in the mountains to the north. One of them had
to stay behind to watch over the women, although it was common
enough knowledge that the women were actually quite capable of
looking after themselves. Lots were drawn and the task of staying
with the women fell to Garaidh who, though he was a fine and
experienced warrior, adept in both battle and the hunt, was vain.
He was extremely proud of his long, golden hair which he wore in
braids which he was often to be seen combing and braiding. Most
of the ancient tribal warriors of Scotland wore their hair long and
had moustaches which necessitated a deal of care – but Garaidh
was a bit of a poser.

After the warriors left for the hunt in the morning Garaidh,
considerably put out at missing the hunt, combed and braided his
hair as the women went about their daily business. As the day
wore on it got hotter and hotter and Garaidh eventually stretched
himself on the ground outside the fort and fell asleep. The women,
seeing him lying there with this long braids carefully spread on the
ground around his head, decided to play a trick on him. A couple
of them sneaked up on the sleeping warrior and proceeded to pin
each of his braids securely in the ground with hammers and pegs.
Then, retreating back inside the fort, closing and barring the gate,
they gave a great shout. Garaidh leapt to his feet, drawing his

sword and adopting a defensive posture all in the one movement. His long glorious braids were torn from his head and blood was streaming from his torn scalp. He let out a great roar. The women were looking over the fort wall, pointing and laughing. Garaidh turned to see them and his pain turned to blind rage. He ran and hammered on the gate, but the fort was well-built and the gate stood firm. With the women laughing and jeering his anger and hurt pride could only grow. He ran off, the women hooting after him.

He was back in minutes with great bundles of dry straw and brushwood which he began to heap around the wooden fort. The women, realising his intention was to burn the fort soon stopped laughing and began to tell him to stop. As he continued with his work their demands turned to pleas – after all it had only been a practical joke. Garaidh ignored them. When he had piled enough kindling round the fort, he set fire to it and stood back to watch it burn. It had been a long, dry summer and within seconds flames were licking up the walls of the fort and the palisades themselves soon burst into flame. The cries and the shrieks were horrible and Garaidh took his place in front of the gate sword in hand, ready to strike down any woman who dared try and escape. Soon the entire fort was blazing and the screams of the women died away.

Away in the hills to the northeast Finn and his men were following the trail of a fine boar when Finn himself turned and looked to the southwest. A great plume of smoke rose in the sky from Fendoch. At once he turned and began to run back, followed immediately by the well-trained Fianna. By the time they got to Fendoch there was nothing but a smoking heap of ashes and no sign of Garaidh or any of their wives. Once they saw Garaidh's braids, still pinned to the ground, they deduced what had happened. The grief-stricken Fianna soon set out on a grim hunt for Garaidh who had fled the scene of the crime once his head had cleared and he realised what he had done. They found him in a cave further up Glen Almond and he was killed on the spot.

It is from this time on, we are told, that the end of the Fianna was in sight: there were no women Fianna left and there could be no more children of the Fianna. This is why we no longer have such magnificent giants in Scotland.

# The Muileartach

Earlier we learned the extent of goddess tales in Scotland's land-scape, most of these represented as giant females. One such was the Muileartach of Mull. The Muileartach is said to have walked out of the sea to approach Finn's dwelling. On the way, she pulled up a tree, swept off the branches and used it for a stick. She came to Finn's door and begged to be let in, claiming to be nothing but a poor old woman wanting to warm herself at the fire. Now Finn could understand everything by biting his thumb, which he burned by the Salmon of Knowledge when he was a child. So biting his thumb he realised who was at the door and refused to open it. At this the Muilertach showed her true colours and kicked the door in, snatching Finn's famous Cup of Victory. This vessel was a magic cup which gave mysterious powers to Finn as well as being able to magically feed the Fianna. Two of the Fianna, Caoilte and Oscar chased her and regained the cup after a short fight.

Another story on Mull relates how one day the Muileartach was returning from a journey to the north. She had one foot on Mull and one on the Ardnamurchan peninsula, straddling the Sound of Mull (A20). In this awkward position a ship came sail-ing through the sound, causing her to lose her balance, fall into the water and drown. She must have been a giant for the Sound of Mull is nearly two kilometres wide at its narrowest point, but what size must the ship have been to coup such a giantess?

# The Making of the Outer Hebrides

An old tale tells us that long, long ago, before the clans had been formed or the druids had worshipped at stone circles and before even the Outer Hebrides were formed, a great giant lived in Stack Rock, far out in the Western Sea. This terrifying and enormous giant had nine heads and nine mouths, each with a fearsome appetite. His preferred dish was young women and he was in the habit of raiding Inner isles like Skye, Raasay, Rum (A27) and Eigg, stealing maidens, nine at a time. He would then take them back to his castle and each would be a meal for one of his nine mouths.

One day he had made a successful raid on Skye and was heading home through the ocean, unaware that one of his captives was promised in marriage to a young man of great character. Refusing to mourn for his stolen fiancée, the young hero went into the Cuillinns to ask help from a kelpie that lived in an isolated lochan. After some bargaining the kelpie agreed to help and the pair of them set off to Stack Rock. Though the fight was long and hard, they finally managed to cut off eight of the giant's great ugly heads. This weakened the monster enough for the hero to kill him with a thrust to the heart. He then released his intended and her companions who were all very grateful for their release. Before returning to Skye they wondered what to do with the giant's body and eight heads. There was not sufficient ground on Stack Rock to bury him so pieces of the great cadaver were thrown into the sea, where they floated. The hero and the nine maidens all mounted on the broad back of the kelpie and headed back to Skye.

Well, the sea is great and proved capable of dealing with this monster. Birds began to descend in flocks upon the body of the giant just as shoals of fish swam to it under the waves. Soon the body of the vast monster was reduced to bones. Even these remains were too large simply to wear away and there they lay lashed by wind and rain, giving shelter to birds and fish until they merged with the flotsam and jetsam of the sea and vast fields of sea-wrack. The body formed itself into the cliffs and rocks of the long islands of Harris (A7) and Lewis (A5), North and South Uist (A10), Benbecula and Barra (A14). Even today you can see the outline of the giant in the shape of these isles with the last head the Butt of Lewis (A1) and the soles of his feet forming the cliffs of South Bernera (A16). His eight heads became the islands of Bernera, Eriskay (A13), Mingualay (A15), Vallay, Gramsay, Taransay (A6), Pabbay (A8) and Killegray (A9), although they are of different sizes.

## Guru

A tale of a giantess from Sutherland may be a remnant of Norse mythology. This part of Scotland was ruled by the King of

Norway until the sixteenth century and many Norse people settled in the seven hundred years before then.

Guru was a giantess who came to Sutherland from Norway with her husband when the old Norse gods fled before the coming of Christianity, around 1,000 AD. They set themselves up on an island in a loch not far from Forsinard (B5). Being giants from the pagan world they had no souls and thus there was no real place for them in Christendom. One day they heard that St Olaf had sent some missionaries to Sutherland to convert the local pagans. Soon they saw one coming out to their island in a boat. Without coming ashore, he told them that their home would provide the perfect location for the church he intended building and asked them to leave. They told him to be on his way. Guru's husband walked into the loch, lifted up the boat and threw it to the far

Guru

shore with the priest still in it. The saint raised his cross in retaliation and turned the giant into a pillar of stone.

Guru was distraught and began weeping and crying about how good her man had been to her as well as to all the local humans. The priest, perhaps beginning to have second thoughts about his rash action, went off and consulted with the local populace. None had a bad word to say about the now petrified giant. So the priest then made a concession: the giant might come back to life for one night a year if embraced by one of his own kind who would be prepared to give up a hundred years of his or her own life to do so. The distraught Guru agreed to this deal and soon the priest left to convert pagans somewhere else. But he kept his word: every year at yuletide Guru and her husband were re-united.

Then one year a young couple landed on the island begging shelter. Guru said they could stay there in her island, as long as they went away each Yuletide and this they agreed to. A year or two later the young lass, named Astog, became pregnant; the baby was due in midwinter.

Astog's child was born on Christmas Eve. Guru could not bring herself to turn the young mother and the new-born child out. She made the lass and her husband promise not to look outside or mention the Holy Name at all on Christmas Day. But as the day wore on the child began to cry and the lass shushed her and blessed her unthinkingly. Guru's husband had been flesh until that moment but was now immediately turned back into stone – forever. Guru let out a heart-rending scream. With her husband gone for good she could not bear to live on the island any longer. She gave it to Astog and her husband on the condition they treated a local group of hill-dwarves with kindness. She went off to live out her life wandering the face of the earth.

A few years later St Olaf's priest returned to the district to find that paganism had reasserted itself. He wondered why his preaching of God's love had had so little success in the area.

## Fear Liath Mor

Ben Macdui (B34) is Scotland's second highest mountain. It is the highest of the Cairngorms, the highest section of the Grampian Mountains, an area known for startling beauty and sudden life-threatening changes in weather patterns. Over the years many people have lost their lives in these mountains and many others have come close to death. Some of these have come across Fear Liath Mor, the Big Grey Man of Ben Macdui. As all who have tramped the mountain tops in mist can tell, the senses will shift, and even familiar features can take on strange and eerie aspects. Small rock faces can suddenly seem like vast walls, and cairns and scarps can loom out of the mist like great beasts crouching to spring. But there is more to Fear Liath Mor than this.

There are those who believe that he is a malevolent spirit on the lookout for lone climbers with the intention of driving them over Lurcher's Gully into the pass of Lairig Ghru (B33) far below. Several people have reported hearing footsteps following them as they crossed the plateau – one footstep to every three or four of their own – and there are numerous sightings of a vast grey

Fear Liath Mor

creature looming out of the mist. Still others have reported a malignant force pushing them towards Lurcher's Gully. Others have heard roaring voices followed by crunching footsteps in the snow, and some have felt that there was a whole race of beings atop the Cairngorms. There have even been reports of huge footsteps seen in the snow. Sometimes one person sees or senses something while a companion senses nothing. But all these events have happened in the mist when normal sense and hearing are considerably altered. Mist seems to bend the light, deaden sound and then amplify it as winds whirl and the moisture condenses or dissipates. There has also been a 'rational' explanation – the apparition is said to be a natural phenomenon, the Brocken Spectre. Named for a German mountain, this phenomenon is no more than one's own shadow greatly enlarged in the mist. Those who have walked the Scottish mountains in mist know, however, that life itself seems very different in the cold damp surroundings and the world seems no more than a few yards across. Local people in the straths and glens of Rothiemurchus simply accept that the Big Grey Man is up there.

The lore of these giants and the massive Fianna was an important part of the process of passing on understanding of the physical world and the necessary rules of society that had been handed down through the generations by word of mouth. As to whether giants actually existed, there have been reports of giant skeletons in the past and there might yet be surprises in store for us.

# CHAPTER 10

# Stone Circles and Standing Stones

ALL OVER SCOTLAND WE find standing stones. Sometimes one stands alone in a field. In other cases, we find a circle of stones in now out of the way locations. While we know that many of these erections were raised in the Stone Age, we have no definite idea of their use. The effort required to raise some of the larger stones illustrates their importance – not to mention their organising and transporting. Although we are learning that the lives of hunter-gatherers and early agriculturists were not as difficult and wearisome as they were once thought to be, it is clear they put hard work into erecting these stones.

Much romanticised speculation has been written over the years concerning druids, stone circles and standing stones. The druids, first of all, existed thousands of years after the stones were raised – and it is unlikely they formed an organised movement in any case. But these myth-based ideas on origin are interesting. One such comes from a man called Donovan, a diviner working and living in Dartmoor in southwest England. He said he dowsed the same sort of patterns below stone circles as he found at deer rutting sites. Donovan suggested that early people, seeing the deer return year after year to mate at the same sites, began to associate such locations with fertility and the ongoing turn of the seasons and began to raise their own sacred sites there.

Other scholars, like the late Alexander Thom, have concentrated 'on the mathematics and astronomical alignments of the circles, suggesting common units of measurement and a widespread awareness of astronomy at some level. The idea that our ancestors watched the stars turning in the heavens makes sense, and it is easy to believe that some of the circles were in some way arranged in relation to the position of the moon and particularly bright stars or planets. Recumbent stone circles with a flat horizontal stone in their southeast quadrants, are unique to northeast Scotland and might have been associated with the moon.

In the Gaelic oral tradition many of these stones are known as fir bhreige, false men. The story is that a group of people, ignoring warnings from their priests, decided to play music and dance on the Sabbath. When they were in the height of revelry they were suddenly transformed into stone in punishment. This story was told of the great circle of Calanais (A4) in Lewis as well as many others and seems to have been an attempt to keep people away from the stones. The idea is common all over the United Kingdom. What we can say is that the stones themselves must have held a strong attraction for the Church to come up with this explanation of their creation.

## Clach Ossian

It is possible, if unproveable, that some of the beliefs and practices associated with the ancient standing stones and circles stem from the time they were erected, roughly 3,000 – 1,000 BC. Belief in such sites is tenacious, remaining in place for thousands of years sometimes – as in the case of Clach Ossian, the Stone of Ossian. This massive great boulder lies just off the road in the Sma Glen, a few miles north of Crieff in Strathearn.

Clach Ossian

In the 1730s the London government was making a concerted attempt to open up the Highlands and change the way of life of the clanspeople, still living much as their Iron Age ancestors had two thousand years before. Although the clan system was breaking down in the face of the new money economy and increasing governmental centralization, people still held to the old beliefs. General Wade had been put in charge of driving highways along the old drove roads into the Highlands and one autumn in the mid-1730s his engineers, with accompanying military escort, were pushing the road through the Sma Glen. Right in the way of the new road there stood a massive boulder on a raised area. Using the technology of the day, levers and combined horse and manpower, the army engineers managed to move the stone off to the side. Then there was sudden consternation as it was realised there was a pit below where the stone had stood. And in the pit was an ancient urn. The officers in charge called an immediate halt to work and word was sent back to General Wade that they had found a Roman burial! The officers knew all about the Romans, fine models that they were for the expanding British Empire, but knew little or nothing of Scotland's past. A guard was set over to the burial as work finished for the day and the soldiers and engineers went back down to Fendoch, itself the reputed site of a Fianna fort. The guard settled down for the night. A couple of hours later he noticed a procession of torches coming towards him from the south; the sound of bagpipes echoed through the glen. The eerie lights grew closer and well before the crowd reached the stone he had given up all thought of protecting the archaeological site, orders or not. The torches were carried by a substantial crowd of local people amongst whom were the kilted soldiers from the Highland regiment. Many of these people were Gaelic speakers and although they might not have been able to read, they knew the great stories of Finn Mac Cuill. These formed part of the great treasury of Gaelic lore which fired the European success of James McPherson at the end of the century. His Ossianic poems drew from the same well that was inspiring these people, for they knew who was buried under the great stone. For generations it had been told that this was the final resting place of Ossian himself who had transformed the heroic deeds of Finn and the Fianna into poetry and song. Ossian had been Finn's son and long believed to have outlived his fellow Fianna. The people had come to pay their respects – and more.

The urn was raised from the pit and carried reverently to the top of nearby Dunmore (D33), a piper playing. Here, within a hill-fort believed to have been occupied by the Fianna themselves, the ashes were ceremoniously laid to rest. The locals left, their work completed.

In all likelihood the urn and its ashes were much earlier than the time when tribes like the mythological Fianna may have lived – what little we know suggests a Stone Age origin. However the sanctity of the site itself and respect for whoever was buried there had clearly continued through linguistic and societal changes. The reverence of the people for their culture had lead them to intervene directly in what they saw as a sacrilegious act and they had made sure their great hero was safe from further disturbance. To this day no one knows exactly where the ashes were reburied.

This type of linkage between Stone Age monuments and the heroic saga of the Fianna happened elsewhere, too. (In one sense, this is hardly surprising, since there is no evidence to show that the population of Scotland has ever been totally overrun by invaders.) The standing stones and circles were erected by the ancestors of the people who became the Highland and Lowland clans – and today's Scots.

## *The Stone of Odin*

A totally different kind of belief was associated with another stone much further north, on Orkney. Here on the main island of Orkney (B3) a few miles north of Kirkwall, are the awesome Stones of Stenness (B2). This ruined stone circle once boasted twelve stones, of which four remain. The circle is 31.1 metres in circumference. Local belief was that this and its partner circle, the larger Ring of Brodgar (142 metres in diameter) were once the sites of sun and moon worship. One of the Stenness stones was particularly noteworthy. This was the Stone of Odin, a six-metre high, one-metre wide and forty-centimetre thick monolith destroyed in 1814, through which there was a hole. Through this hole, lovers would clasp their hands and enter into marriage. (This is a variant on the time-honoured custom of handfasting, a form of marriage by public declaration. Couples who wished to divorce could do so by leaving through separate doors of a church after the service.)

But Odin is none other than the chief god of the Norse pantheon. Norwegian culture was very important in Scotland and not until the sixteenth century did Norwegian kings give up their ownership of Orkney and Shetland. The Shetland dialect of Scots, called Norn, still holds many words and phrases of Norse origin.

The area around the Brodgar and Stenness stones is full of barrows and stone alignments and it is more than probable that the pagan Norsemen in Orkney were using the site much as it had been used millennia before they arrived. Nearby is the magnificent megalithic tomb of Maes Howe (B1) on which tradition is sadly silent. It was raided by Vikings at some point who left runes carved on its walls.

## Deil's Stanes

All over Scotland there are stories of supernatural beings throwing great boulders vast distances. When the Devil throws stones, he is often said to have been aiming at a saint or priest building a church. One of these is the Puddock Stone at Invergowrie (B19), just outside Dundee on the north bank of the River Tay. Tradition tells us that St Boniface was overseeing the building of a church when the devil became aware of him. At the time the devil was walking near St Andrews some twenty miles away. Angered at the saint's presumption, he picked up the stone and threw it at the church. He missed by quite a bit – the Puddock Stone landed half a mile to the north of the church! Also in the area, between the site of the church and Invergowrie Bay (now much reduced due to a policy of landfilling by Dundee City Council) there were also the Goors of Gowrie. These two great monoliths are said to have figured in a rhyme by the seer Thomas the Rhymer: 'When the Goors of Gowrie come to land, Judgement Day is near to hand.' Perhaps the landfilling policy of the nearby city is of more importance than has generally been thought!

Another story of the same type comes from Strathpeffer (B11) in the Highlands and involves Finn Mac Cuill himself. He was staying in a fort on top of Knockfarrel, nowadays overlooking Strathpeffer, when he was challenged to a stone-putting competition by a local giant renowned for his prowess. The mighty Finn felt this a bit beneath his dignity so he offered to pit his dwarf against Stoneputter. The competition took place on Knockfarrel itself. The giant lifted a stone which three men together could not lift and he threw it into the valley. This was the Eagle Stone, the Pictish symbol stone just to the east of the village. Then it was the dwarf's turn. He went to the gateposts of the old fort of Knockfarrel, each of which was too heavy for seven men to lift, and threw them singly to stand on either side of the Eagle stone. Even Finn's dwarf was superior to the local giant! The proof of the story is that one of these stones supposedly has the marks of a finger and thumb on it.

## Granish Moor

On Granish Moor (B26) just north of Aviemore there is a small loch called Loch nan Carraigean (B27), loch of the stones, where a tradition which may have inspired the witch scene in Shakespeare's Macbeth.

Granish Moor

The freshly-crowned king of the Picts was said to have come to consult at this circle of stones with the three women who lived there. The spirits were then raised by some kind of ritual and asked about the future of his reign. The Picts are often presented as a semi-fictitious group, but they were simply a people otherwise referred to as Caledonians who inhabited Scotland from the time of the Romans until the ninth century. At that point, they merged with Gaelic-speaking Scots to form the new kingdom of Scotland. Macbeth, who seems to have been an honourable and efficient king with an excellent claim to the throne of Scotland, came from Moray, long the heartland of the northern Picts and a continuing source of trouble for the centralizing Scottish kings of the early Middle Ages. Presumably it was the kings or leaders of these tribes who came to Loch nan Carraigean.

## Lang Man's Grave

In the lonely glen below Macbeth's one-time castle on Dunsinane (D21) there is a strange stone with an even stranger story attached to it. The stone, which once appears to have been a standing stone, is lying on the ground on the north side of the road from Balbeggie to Abernyte, just east of the burn which runs down between Dunsinane and Black Hill. The stone itself lies under the roadside dyke. For many years the roadmen cleaned the small gravel bed surrounding the stone on the roadside to show respect for our ancient traditions. The stone is associated with the Lang Man, a weel-kennt and successful horse trader who regularly visited the annual fair held in the glen. Standing about two metres tall he was a gregarious character and one of the great delights of the fair was said to be having a dram with the Lang Man. Tradition does not give us a date for the story but we are told that one year the Lang Man disappeared and when the fair was over his tent still stood, his horse tethered beside it. Of the Lang Man himself there was no sign. There had been no suggestion of trouble or violence beyond the normal drunken boisterousness of the fair, so rumours of witchcraft ran rife. No one was prepared to take down his tent, though the horse was soon appropriated. The wind and weather came to destroy the flapping canvas of his tent and the tale began to spread that he had been murdered for his poke o gowd and buried beneath the great stone lying by the road. Perhaps we will never know if anyone lies in the Lang Man's Grave (D22) but its proximity to Dunsinane and the reverence shown to the stone itself have led to suggestions that this is where the original Stone of Destiny was buried when it was taken away from Scone at the approach of the English army in 1296.

## Calanais

One of the most remarkable megalithic structures in Britain and Ireland stands overlooking Loch Roag (A3) on the western side of the Isle of Lewis. This is the unique stone circle of Calanais. The landscape around it is dotted with many more megalithic sites, showing that this was an area of major importance five thousand years ago. The location of the site by a sea loch at one of the western fringes of Europe reminds us that travel by water was commonplace then, and much easier than travel across the heavily wooded land mass of the continent. The monument is roughly in the shape of a Celtic cross: there is a central circle, a long avenue running north/south and shorter avenues leading from the circle to east and west, although the original design is no longer totally extant, some stones having disappeared.

Calanais is ideally positioned to see the standstill of the moon. This is the time every 18.6 years that the moon reaches its furthest west setting. At that time, it can be seen clearly from the notch of hills south of the avenue of Calanais. The hills to the south are Cailich na Mointich, discussed above with reference to the shape of a sleeping woman.

When Martin Martin visited the island in 1695 he was told that the site had been a place of worship in heathen times. He was not the first to write of this

Calanais

mysterious and awesome place however. An ancient Greek writer wrote of a priest called Abaris who came to Athens around 350 AD from 'the winged temple of Apollo' in Hyperborea. Hyperborea means 'place beyond the north wind' and is generally agreed to refer to the British Isles. Many scholars feel that the reference is specifically to Stonehenge, but Calanais is a much better fit. The god Apollo was said to dance at this temple every nineteen years and we have already seen how Calanais was created to watch the 18.6 year cycle of the moon. But Apollo is a sun god, anyway. And here the local legends of Calanais begin to matter. Each Midsummer 'the shining one' is said to walk down the central avenue of Calanais. He is heralded by a cuckoo (and it was thought that all cuckoos visiting Lewis first flew to Calanais). While 'the shining one' is usually though to be Lugh, it might also be a reference to Apollo.

A legend concerning the erection of the stones was written down by a local minister last century and it tells of a group of ships coming into Loch Roag manned by black men. They were accompanied by priests, the chief of whom had a white cloak of bird feathers. After the stones were erected, the ships and their crews left but the priests stayed behind to officiate at the stones. All we know by way of background to this tale is that the megalith builders seemed to have sailed up the coast of Europe from as far south as Morocco. All the Atlantic coastal lands have great stone creations and it is intriguing that many of them are from Morocco.

Calanais has attracted other types of more general stories through its long existence. One story says that local giants met to discuss what to do about the arrival of a Christian missionary – St Kieran – who turned them into stone once they had all gathered!

Another story tells of a great white cow that came to the stones from Loch Roag in a time of hardship and near famine after a Viking raid on the island. No matter how often she was milked this cow gave freely to everyone who brought a pail. One day a woman came with two pails and the cow asked her (in Gaelic) what she was doing. The woman explained that her friend was sick and had asked her to bring her pail for milk. So the cow let her have two pails' worth of milk. This was noticed by another woman, who happened to be a greedy witch. She brought two buckets the next day, but the cow realised what was happening and only let her have the one. Angered by this, the spiteful witch returned the following day with one pail – but it was a pail with no bottom. In this way she milked the cow dry and the magical creature disappeared, never to be seen again.

Another local tale of witchcraft concerns two young women who were in love with the same man. They had been friends but were now being driven apart. One of them went to consult a witch as to how she could ensure her success. The witch gave her a magic belt which she was to give to her rival. She would then be taken away by her 'master' – the Devil. The lass accepted the belt but began to realise what she was doing; she decided against harming her friend. But how could she get rid of her belt?

She went on her own late one evening to the stones of Calanais. Summoning all her courage, she took the belt and fastened it around one of the stones. The stone burst into flame and the air was filled with a great noise of howling and honking and the flapping of wings. A great cloud of smoke began to gather and the lass took to her heels. But the next day she returned. The stone round which she had fastened the belt was broken just above where it had been clasped and the upper half of it lay on the ground with scorch marks at the break. This is believed to be the stone just outside the circle on the east side of the southern avenue, given as number 34 in some descriptions.

The range of stories relating to Calanais is hardly surprising. When you first see them along the ridge at Breasclete (A2) they take your breath away. As more and more sites in the locality are discovered, the fundamental importance of this magical place is underlined.

Standing stones and circles have been associated with many kinds of activity over the past few decades. Some people see them as markers on a system of ley lines – lines of electro-magnetic power that run vast distances across the landscape, absolutely straight. Others think of them as some kind of geo-physical acupuncture for the planet. Still others think they provide the focus for extraterrestrial activity, while others use them for their own version of re-invented paganism. What this clearly illustrates is that these megalithic remnants have lost none of their psychological attraction for us. The legends associated with them show just how divergent the rituals and beliefs associated with them have been.

CHAPTER II

# Wells, Trees and Sacred Groves

WATER IS BASIC TO SCOTLAND. We have lochs, rivers, wells and springs – and rain in all our seasons. But water is also the bearer of sanctity and is involved in the rituals of many religions. Christians use water for baptism and christening. Water was also at the heart of various earlier religions. The association of goddess-type figures with our rivers attests to this. In pagan times water may have been seen as the blood of a goddess.

In Scotland many well-rituals survived into the nineteenth and twentieth centuries, giving us glimpses of how our ancestors saw themselves in the world. Many of these wells have been, and some continue to be, associated with healing.

## *Nine Maidens Wells*

We have read about Martin's Stane and the nine maidens. The same nine crop up in other locations and an almost identical story is told of a well at Kildrummy (B50) near Castle Forbes in Aberdeenshire. Here the founder of Clan Forbes, a Pictish warrior called Ochonochar, slew a great wild boar which had also killed nine maidens. Other nine maidens wells can be found at Cortachy, (D8) Finavon (D10), Glamis (D13), Newburgh (D45), Tough (B49) and Pitsligo (B23), Loch Tay, Parkside (by Murrayshall (D24)) and in Abernethy on the south of the Tay, east of Perth. There is a possibility that many of the Ninewells that exist all across Scotland were at one time nine maidens wells, though there are other valid interpretations of the name. At Abernethy, the nine maidens were said to be the companions of St Brigit who came over from Ireland at the request of the Pictish king to set up a nunnery.

The motif of the nine maidens exists in the mythology and lore

115

of most Western European countries, possibly linking such diverse figures as King Arthur, the Norse Gods Heimdall and Odin, Apollo and the Welsh St Samson of Dol.

## Bride's Wells

Bride (and St Brigit) were often associated with well-rituals. One such survived until recently at Bride's Well at Sanquhar (C3) in the Southwest. Here, young women would go to the well at Beltane and place nine white stones in it. (The link to the nine maidens theme is attractive, but the use of white pebbles is equally striking. White pebbles were used by both pagans and early Christians as talismans to be placed into graves.)

Nine Maidens Well

There are Bride's Wells all over Scotland from Wigton (C1) to Aberdeen and one particular one at Pitlochry was said to provide a cure for respiratory diseases. Another Bride's Well at Corgarrf, between Braemar and Tomintoul, was a favourite spot for brides. On the evening before their marriages it was customary for young girls to go to the well with their bridesmaids and bathe the bride's feet and the upper parts of her body with water from the well. It was believed that this bathing would ensure the girl a family.

## Clootie Well

The best-known Clootie Well (B13) is on the Black Isle. Here, the trees on both sides of the well alongside the road are draped with rags. This is a remnant of belief in a healing well. A rag would be tied by a sufferer to the holy tree beside the well and as the rag faded so the affliction would disappear. This applied to sicknesses of the heart and mind as well as of the body. It was also acceptable for people to take rags on behalf of others too ill to move. Of course anyone mad enough to remove or meddle with the rags

Clootie Well

would fall heir to all the diseases represented! Such practices were widespread and a particularly well-known Clootie Well is on Culloden Moor, sadly famous for other things.

Like so many of the healing wells, this one was visited at Beltane. It seems that such pilgrimages could become great social occasions in which, as in pagan times, religious practice and revelry would be totally intermingled. The Clootie Well on Culloden (B14) was also known as St Mary's Well, The Blue Well and Tobar n'Oige, or well of youth. This last name suggests a link to that fabulous land Tír na nÓg, the land of youth which occurs in early Gaelic literature and folklore. The ritual at this well is likely to have been pretty much consistent with that performed at others. The pilgrim would walk three times 'sunwise' (clockwise) round the well then drink from it with cupped hands while making his wish or prayer. Then a piece of silver would be thrown into the well. Finally the pilgrim would tie a rag of clothing to the branch of the overhanging tree or bush. This was thought by some to immediately remove all ill-health. The entire ritual had to be performed in silence before the sun rose. Certain wells have updated ancient practice and have charity boxes for donations.

# Eye Wells

Many wells in Scotland are said to have been a particular source of remedies for ocular ailments. Some of these 'eye wells' are dedicated to early saints like St Triduana and St Monenna. The latter was said to have been accompanied by nine maidens and a boy. The stories of St Triduana and St Monenna are essentially the same. St Triduana despite having entered the sisterhood of nuns and dedicating her life to Jesus, was pursued by an ardent suitor who, in true early Christian style, was of royal descent. Try as she might, she could not escape from him. She moved several times but still he came after her, despite her strict vow of chastity. At last she asked him what it was about her that most attracted him. On being told that he was enflamed by her beautiful eyes she simply plucked them out and gave them to the astonished prince. This is said to be why certain wells were said to be good for the eyes. St Triduana's Well in Edinburgh was originally at Restalrig Church in Edinburgh but was moved to a location in Holyrood Park (D58) where it can still be seen opposite Holyrood Palace. What is truly remarkable about St Monenna is that she is reported to have had churches dedicated to her on Traprain Law (D55) in East Lothian, Edinburgh Castle Rock (D59), Stirling Castle Rock (D37), Dumbarton (C9) and Dundonald (C4) in Ayrshire. All of these were heavily fortified sites and almost certainly tribal capitals in the Dark Ages.

# Moving Wells

On the island of Islay there is a well that is said to have originated on Colonsay (C20). One day a local woman went to the well and washed her hands in it. This sacrilegious act was outrageous and the well immediately spirited itself away to Islay where ever after it was properly respected and was the site of numerous pilgrimages.

Another version of the same story tells that the well was brought to Islay by Donald, Lord of the Isles, when he moved from Colonsay to Finlaggan (C21) in Islay. Other movable wells seem to have shifted for the same kind of reason but there is one story of a moving well that takes some beating.

The story is from Strath Dearn (B24), southeast of Inverness (B15). A man who had been raised here by the headwaters of the Findhorn River grew old watching his friends and relatives leave their beloved Highlands for a better life on the Canadian prairies. Despite regular invitations he declined to follow them and lived on in Strath Dearn. One of the things that kept him there was his attachment to the well near his birthplace which had supplied him with water all his days. However, after many years his relatives at last convinced him to go to Canada. He went to the well for the last time and sat on the large white rock where he often read his Bible. He was still thinking of the spot when he arrived in Canada. And there, just a few yards from his new home was his faithful well and the white boulder waiting for him.

## The Queen and the Well

Wells are magic in many ways and crop up in all sorts of stories. This one comes from Port Ellen (C22) on Islay. One day the queen fell ill and told the eldest of her daughters to go to the Well of True Water to bring her a drink. She was sure that this would restore her to health. On reaching the Well of True Water the young princess was approached by a large frog who asked her to marry him. She was mortally offended at the suggestion and said she would never do such a thing. 'Well then,' said the toad, 'You'll not get any water.'

On returning home without the water the queen was angry and sent the girl's younger sister to the well instead. The same thing happened to the second sister as had happened to the first and she too came home without any water.

By this time the queen was very ill. In desperation she sent her youngest daughter to the Well of True Water to bring her a drink. When she got there the frog appeared again and asked the third sister if she would marry him. On being told that this was the only way he would let her have the water for her mother, the lass agreed to wed the frog. He gave her the water and she ran off at once to her mother. The queen drank the water and immediately felt better.

The Queen and the frog

That night after all were in bed, the frog came to the front of their dwelling and called to the youngest sister: 'Gentle one, gentle one, remember the pledge you gave me beside the well, my love.' He kept repeating this over and over and at last the princess came down and let him in, putting him behind the door. She went back to bed but soon was awakened by the frog repeating that same phrase over and over again. So she took him into her chamber and put him down there. It was not long before he started again, repeating and repeating the same phrase. She then made him a wee bed right by the fire hoping this would quieten him. But again he started and this time she made him up a bed alongside her own. Yet again he started but she decided enough was enough and decided to ignore him.

At that his chant stopped and he said to her, 'There is an old rusty sword behind your bed. Lift it up and cut off my head, rather than that this torture should go on.'

So she took up the old rusty sword and with a clean stroke cut off the frog's head. Then there in front of her stood a handsome young man. He told her his story: he was a king from a nearby kingdom who had been put under a spell and as she had saved his life by agreeing to marry him they could now be wed. The young princess was very taken by the handsome stranger and soon they were married and had a long and happy life together.

## Katherine's Well

As we have seen, the pre-Reformation church was quite amenable to absorbing earlier religious practices into its own rituals. A striking example of this comes from Eigg (A26).

In the late eighteenth century Martin Martin toured the Western Isles leaving us a remarkable record of his journey. According to him the water from the well on Eigg, known as Katherine's Well, was believed locally to be extremely beneficial. The natives told Martin that it had been so ever since being blessed by Father Hugh, a Catholic priest. He had gathered all of the inhabitants of the island at the well and got them to raise a huge cairn at the head of the well. He then blessed the well and gave all present a small piece of candle which they lit. The priest then led the assembled throng in single file 'sunwise' round the well. From then on it was sacrilege to use the water of the well for cooking.

This is clearly a remnant of an early practice which some priests saw as useful. Most wells were believed to be at the peak of their powers on Beltane or one of the other feast days – Samhain (1 November), Imbolc (1 February), or Lammas (1 August).

The modern idea of the 'wishing' well is clearly derived from this kind of ancient idea of supplication. One of the ongoing concerns in society in older times was fertility and there were many locations which were thought to have the power to make barren women fertile, or at least encourage the possibility of pregnancy. Naturally, some of these sites were wells.

## The Well in Willie's Muir

John R. Allan was told the following story in the 1920s by an old man who saw the ritual when he himself was a young lad. The well concerned was located in an area called Willie's Muir in Aberdeenshire.

The well was in a sheltered dip on the moor and the water came out among some stones surrounded by whin-bushes. Three women of child-bearing age went to the well at Midsummer accompanied by an older woman who was clearly the one in charge. The young lad followed them, keeping in cover all the while.

On reaching the well and with instruction from the older woman, the three others took off their shoes and stockings and pulled their skirts and petticoats up to bare their bellies. They then circled the well three times sunwise, holding up their skirts as if holding themselves towards the sun. As they came round, the old woman cupped water from the well and splashed each one's genitalia with it. Not a word was spoken, even though the water must have been gey cold. Three times round they went and then the old woman made a sign. The women dropped their skirts and petticoats. Then they opened their dresses to the waist and pulled them down, freeing their breasts. At another sign from the Auld Wife, they knelt before her and this time she took the spring water and sprinkled it over their breasts three time three. Then they adjusted their clothing, put on their stockings and shoes and left. This report probably dates from the middle of the nineteenth century.

## Sacred Trees

As mentioned above, the ancient holy wells were usually adjoined by one or more trees. The famous well of St Mourie on Isle Maree has such a tree which pilgrims used to shove or hammer coins in as a token of respect and to have good luck. There are stories of wells in Argyll that have nine hazel trees growing around them still. This is an echo of this motif in both Irish and Scottish Gaelic tales of the Well of Knowledge. This mystical well was surrounded by nine hazel trees whose nuts bore the sum of human knowledge. The nuts would fall into the pool and in the pool was a salmon who fed on the nuts, thus becoming immensely knowledgeable.

Trees can be significant either as individual entities or in groves and there are said to have been many trees that were seen as particularly sacred by the tribal peoples of Britain. The best known of these is the oak, with its links to the shadowy figures of the druids. There are records of mistletoe cut at Samhain being used to ward off witchcraft or to protect children form being stolen by fairies.

## The Rowan

The most widely respected tree in Scotland was the rowan. Its berries were said to have been the food of the gods but its particular strength was in warding off evil. The wood of the rowan was used for the pins of ploughs, millstones, churn-staffs and pegs of cow-shackles. It was also common for the central cross-beam in the chimneys of old houses to be made of rowan. The term could also be used for the main roofbeam of a house. To ward off evil from one's cattle it was common to put a sprig of rowan over the byre door or even to tie sprigs of it to cow's tails, but always with red thread. An old rhyme tells of the efficacy of using red thread of wool, silk or linen, with the rowan:

Rowan tree an red threid
Gar the witches tyne their speed.

Rowan would only be used as firewood for the neid-fire or ritual cooking at Beltane and other special times. The rowan or rodden tree was used at Beltane extensively. It has long been thought of as the most effective plant against witchcraft and black magic, which is why there is hardly a house in the Highlands that did not have a rowan tree growing at its front door at one time. With the depletion of the population of the Highlands solitary rowans may be seen on a hillside or in a glen where all that remains of a house is a rickle of stones.

## The Yew

Perhaps the most significant of our indigenous trees is the yew. The great placename scholar W.J. Watson has suggested that the name 'Iona' derives from 'island of yews'. Throughout Scotland there are kirkyards with yews not only in them but even enclosed by yews or with yew-arches at their entrance. Perhaps the yew contains some active healing ingredient we have forgotten, as many of the sacred trees seem to have. Another possibility is that extracts of certain nuts or fruits could have been used to induce visionary trances. The reverence for the yew might derive from something much more obvious. It is a remarkably long-lived tree and as such could be seen to signify immortality or rebirth in either a pagan or Christian context.

## Sacred Groves

The Romans wrote of nemetons, or sacred groves, in these islands and elsewhere. The name is reminiscent of Gaelic neimheadh, a sacred enclosure. The term was often used for precisely those previously sacred grounds in which so many early churches were raised. These nemetons were sacred spots which probably had judicial or social functions. They can be found in most areas of Scotland – Roseneath (c10) on the Gareloch, Nevay in Angus, Navidale (b7) in Sutherland, Slocknvata in the Rhinns of Galloway, Navitie in Fife and Craig Neimhidh in Glenurquhart.

Another of these ancient sites was Tarnavie (d43). This is a large mound nestling under Craig Rossie (d42) on the south side of Strathearn near Dunning (d44), one of the places where St Serf slew a dragon. The name Tarnavie was long thought to have come from terra navis, or ship of land, because of the shape of the hill: it is a bit like an upturned boat. There is an interesting tale about this site. At a date that no one has ever been certain about, a local farmer came to Tarnavie to dig up some sand. He knew he could get what he wanted there, perhaps because it was initially a drumlin, a mound caused by riverine action. He proceeded to dig. He had hardly started when in front of him he saw a very small man dressed in an old and outlandish style. The strange man asked him what he was doing and on being told replied, 'How would you feel if someone came along and started throwing the slates off your roof? You are disturbing my home. Begone with you now.'

At that the wee man simply sank back into the hill and the farmer turned to his heels and ran. He never set foot on Tarnavie again.

Whether this is a tale intended to frighten people off or to remind them of a fairy hill we cannot be sure. It is very like the ideas we looked at in chapter 1, here linked directly to a name suggesting if not a sacred grove of trees, at least a sacred site or enclosure of some kind. Interestingly, Tomnahurich, which we looked at earlier, is Gaelic for hill of the yew trees. Folktales often contain ancient ideas of sanctity and reference to old holy sites in our landscape.

# Conclusion

THERE IS AN OLD SAYING THAT GOES, 'Gin ye dinnae ken whaur ye've been, hou can ye tell whaur ye're gangin?' This can be translated as, you must know where you've been if you want to know where you're going. In today's electronic world the media seems to be ever more obsessed with what is going to happen tomorrow. Cultures from all over the world are pillaged for 'new' ideas in art, fashion and music. Yet despite this, much survives. As the new century begins, people all over the world will sing Auld Lang Syne, a song given its form by the Scottish poet Rabbie Burns. And as we cross our arms and link hands we will take part in a remnant of an ancient ringdance older than anyone can compute. It is one of the great anomalies of contemporary Scottish society that though the world knows of many aspects of Scottish culture, we are still afraid to teach our ancient history and culture to our children beyond primary school. And all too often all the little ones get is a week of Scots literature around the anniversary of Burns's birth. It seems the senior school curriculum is still dictated by the demands of a defunct empire that equated interest in Scottish culture with a wish for political separatism. The result has been a distorted idea of Scottish history and culture. As long as this continues there will be a reaction against a British view of history that ignores what it does not like and distorts what it cannot ignore.

Despite these problems the interest in our history and our ancient tales continues to grow as does the appreciation of our musical tradition. As interest in old beliefs increases wells are again being visited and we should remember that it is not so long since many of them were the sites of regular pilgrimage and healing visits. We can only learn from our past and hope to understand some of the ways of our ancestors. With a better idea of where we have been perhaps we can create a clearer vision of what we want this Scotland of ours to be.

# Further Reading

BRIGGS, K.M., *British Folk Tales and Legends : A Sampler* 1977

BRUFORD, D. and MacDONALD, D.A., *Scottish Traditional Tales* 1994

CAMERON, I.A., *Highland Chapbook* 1928

CAMPBELL, J.G., *Popular Tales of the West Highlands* 2 vols (reprint) 1994

CAMPBELL, J.G., *More West Highland Tales* 2 vols (reprint) 1994

DOUGLAS, S., *The King of the Black Art and Other Folk Tales* 1987

GREWAR, D., *The Story of Glenisla* 1926

HOPE, A.A., *Midsummer Eve's Dream* 1970

JERVISE, A., *Memorials of Angus and the Mearns* 1861

JERVISE, A., *The Land of the Lindsays* 1882

LEODHAS, SORCHE NIC, *Thistle and Thyme* 1962

LOCHHEAD, MARION, *The Battle of the Birds* 1981

LOCHHEAD, MARION, *Magic and Witchcraft of the Borders* 1984

MacGREGOR, A.A., *The Peat Fire Flame* 1947

MacKENZIE, D.A., *Scottish Folk Lore and Folk Life* 1938

MCNEILL, F. MARIAN, *The Silver Bough* 4 vols (reprint) 1990

MCOWAN, R., *Magic Mountains* 1996

MARSHALL, W., *Historic Scenes in Perthshire* 1879

MILLER, T.D., *Tales of a Highland Parish* 1929

RITCHIE, J., *The Pageant of Moray* 1932

ROSS, A., *The Folklore of the Scottish Highlands* 1976

SIMPSON, E.B., *Folklore of Lowland Scotland* 1976

SWIRE, O., *The Highlands and their Legends* 1963

SWIRE, O., *The Inner Hebrides and their Legends* 1964

SWIRE, O., *The Outer Hebrides and their Legends* 1966

TEMPERLEY, A., *Tales of Galloway* 1979

WATSON, W.J., *The Celtic Placenames of Scotland* (reprint) 1993

WILLIAMSON, DUNCAN & LINDA, *The Thorn in the King's Foot* 1987

WILKIE, J., *Bygone Fife* 1937

WILSON, BARBARA K., *Scottish Folk-tales and Legends* 1954

# Some other books published by **LUATH** PRESS

## FOLKLORE

### The Supernatural Highlands

Francis Thompson

ISBN 0 946487 31 6  PBK  £8.99

An authoritative exploration of the otherworld of the Highlander, happenings and beings hitherto thought to be outwith the ordinary forces of nature. A simple introduction to the way of life of rural Highland and Island communities, this new edition weaves a path through second sight, the evil eye, witchcraft, ghosts, fairies and other supernatural beings, offering new sight-lines on areas of belief once dismissed as folklore and superstition.

### Tall Tales from an Island

Peter Macnab

ISBN 0 946487 07 3  PBK  £8.99

Peter Macnab was born and reared on Mull. He heard many of these tales as a lad, and others he has listened to in later years.

There are humorous tales, grim tales, witty tales, tales of witchcraft, tales of love, tales of heroism, tales of treachery, historical tales and tales of yesteryear.

A popular lecturer, broadcaster and writer, Peter Macnab is the author of a number of books and articles about Mull, the island he knows so intimately and loves so much. As he himself puts it in his introduction to this book 'I am of the unswerving opinion that nowhere else in the world will you find a better way of life, nor a finer people with whom to share it.'

*'All islands, it seems, have a rich store of characters whose stories represent a kind of sub-culture without which island life would be that much poorer. Macnab has succeeded in giving the retelling of the stories a special Mull flavour, so much so that one can visualise the storytellers sitting on a bench outside the house with a few cronies, puffing on their pipes and listening with nodding approval.'* WEST HIGHLAND FREE PRESS

### Tales from the North Coast

Alan Temperley

ISBN 0 946487 18 9  PBK  £8.99

Seals and shipwrecks, witches and fairies, curses and clearances, fact and fantasy – the authen-

tic tales in this collection come straight from the heart of a small Highland community. Children and adults alike responsd to their timeless appeal. These *Tales of the North Coast* were collected in the early 1970s by Alan Temperley and young people at Farr Secondary School in Sutherland. All the stories were gathered from the area between the Kyle of Tongue and Strath Halladale, in scattered communities wonderfully rich in lore that had been passed on by word of mouth down the generations. This wide-ranging selection provides a satisying balance between intriguing tales of the supernatural and more everyday occurrences. The book also includes chilling eye-witness accounts of the notorious Strathnaver Clearances when tenants were given a few hours to pack up and get out of their homes, which were then burned to the ground.

Underlying the continuity through the generations, this new edition has a foreward by Jim Johnston, the head teacher at Farr, and includes the vigorous linocut images produced by the young people under the guidance of their art teacher, Elliot Rudie.

Since the original publication of this book, Alan Temperley has gone on to become a highly regarded writer for children.

*The general reader will find this book's spontaneity, its pictures by the children and its fun utterly charming.* SCOTTISH REVIEW

*An admirable book which should serve as an encouragement to other districts to gather what remains of their heritage of folk-tales.* SCOTTISH EDUCATION JOURNAL

## LUATH GUIDES TO SCOTLAND

These guides are not your traditional where-to-stay and what-to-eat books. They are companions in the rucksack or car seat, providing the discerning traveller with a blend of fiery opinion and moving description. Here you will find *'that curious pastiche of myths and legend and history that the Scots use to describe their heritage... what battle happened in which glen between which clans; where the Picts sacrificed bulls as recently as the 17th century... A lively counterpoint to the more standard, detached guidebook... Intriguing.'* THE WASHINGTON POST

These are perfect guides for the discerning visitor or resident to keep close by for reading again and again, written by authors who invite you to share their intimate knowledge and love of the areas covered.

## Mull and Iona: Highways and Byways

Peter Macnab

ISBN 0 946487 58 8  PBK  £4.95

'The Isle of Mull is of Isles the fairest,
Of ocean's gems 'tis the first and rarest.'
So a local poet described it a hundred years ago, and this recently revised guide to Mull and sacred Iona, the most accessible islands of the Inner Hebrides, takes the reader on a delightful tour of these rare ocean gems, travelling with a native whose unparalleled knowledge and deep feeling for the area unlock the byways of the islands in all their natural beauty.

## South West Scotland

Tom Atkinson

ISBN 0 946487 04 9  PBK  £4.95

This descriptive guide to the magical country of Robert Burns covers Kyle, Carrick, Galloway, Dumfriesshire, Kirkcudbrightshire and Wigtownshire. Hills, unknown moors and unspoiled beaches grace a land steeped in history and legend and portrayed with affection and deep delight.
An essential book for the visitor who yearns to feel at home in this land of peace and grandeur.

## The West Highlands: The Lonely Lands

Tom Atkinson

ISBN 0 946487 56 1  PBK  £4.95

A guide to Inveraray, Glencoe, Loch Awe, Loch Lomond, Cowal, the Kyles of Bute and all of central Argyll written with insight, sympathy and loving detail. Once Atkinson has taken you there, these lands can never feel lonely. 'I have sought to make the complex simple, the beautiful accessible and the strange familiar,' he writes, and indeed he brings to the land a knowledge and affection only accessible to someone with intimate knowledge of the area.

A must for travellers and natives who want to delve beneath the surface.

*'Highly personal and somewhat quirky... steeped in the lore of Scotland.'*
THE WASHINGTON POST

## The Northern Highlands: The Empty Lands

Tom Atkinson

ISBN 0 946487 55 3  PBK  £4.95

The Highlands of Scotland from Ullapool to Bettyhill and Bonar Bridge to John O'Groats are landscapes of myth and legend, 'empty of people, but of nothing else that brings delight to any tired soul,' writes Atkinson. This highly personal guide describes Highland history and landscape with love, compassion and above all sheer magic.
Essential reading for anyone who has dreamed of the Highlands.

## The North West Highlands: Roads to the Isles

Tom Atkinson

ISBN 0 946487 54 5  PBK  £4.95

Ardnamurchan, Morvern, Morar, Moidart and the west coast to Ullapool are included in this guide to the Far West and Far North of Scotland. An unspoiled land of mountains, lochs and silver sands is brought to the walker's toe-tips (and to the reader's fingertips) in this stark, serene and evocative account of town, country and legend.
For any visitor to this Highland wonderland, Queen Victoria's favourite place on earth.

# WALK WITH LUATH

## Mountain Days & Bothy Nights

Dave Brown and Ian Mitchell

ISBN 0 946487 15 4  PBK  £7.50

Acknowledged as a classic of mountain writing still in demand ten years after its first publication, this book takes you into the bothies, howffs and dosses on the Scottish hills. Fishgut Mac, Desperate Dan and Stumpy the Big Yin stalk hill and public house, evading gamekeepers and Royalty with a camaraderie which was the trademark of Scots hillwalking in the early days.

*'The fun element comes through... how innocent the social polemic seems in our nastier world of today... the book for the rucksack this year.'*
Hamish Brown, SCOTTISH MOUNTAINEERING CLUB JOURNAL

## The Joy of Hillwalking

Ralph Storer

ISBN 0 946487 28 6  PBK  £7.50

Apart, perhaps, from the joy of sex, the joy of hillwalking brings more pleasure to more people than any other form of human activity.

*'Alps, America, Scandinavia, you name it – Storer's been there, so why the hell shouldn't he bring all these various and varied places into his observations... [He] even admits to losing his virginity after a day on the Aggy Ridge... Well worth its place alongside Storer's earlier works.'* TAC

## Scotland's Mountains before the Mountaineers

Ian Mitchell

ISBN 0 946487 39 1  PBK £9.99

In this ground-breaking book, Ian Mitchell tells the story of explorations and ascents in the Scottish Highlands in the days before mountaineering became a popular sport – when bandits, Jacobites, poachers and illicit distillers traditionally used the mountains as sanctuary. The book also gives a detailed account of the map makers, road builders, geologists, astronomers and naturalists, many of whom ascended hitherto untrodden summits while working in the Scottish Highlands.

*Scotland's Mountains before the Mountaineers* is divided into four Highland regions, with a map of each region showing key summits. While not designed primarily as a guide, it will be a useful handbook for walkers and climbers. Based on a wealth of new research, this book offers a fresh perspective that will fascinate climbers and mountaineers and everyone interested in the history of mountaineering, cartography, the evolution of landscape and the social history of the Scottish Highlands.

# LUATH WALKING GUIDES

The highly respected and continually updated guides to the Cairngorms.

*'Particularly good on local wildlife and how to see it'* THE COUNTRYMAN

## Walks in the Cairngorms

Ernest Cross

ISBN 0 946487 09 X  PBK  £4.95

This selection of walks celebrates the rare birds, animals, plants and geological wonders of a region often believed difficult to penetrate on foot. Nothing is difficult with this guide in your pocket, as Cross gives a choice for every walker, and includes valuable tips on mountain safety and weather advice.

Ideal for walkers of all ages and skiers waiting for snowier skies.

## Short Walks in the Cairngorms

Ernest Cross

ISBN 0 946487 23 5  PBK  £4.95

Cross wrote this volume after overhearing a walker remark that there were no short walks for lazy ramblers in the Cairngorm region. Here is the answer: rambles through scenic woods with a welcoming pub at the end, bird-watching hints, glacier holes, or for the fit and ambitious, scrambles up hills to admire vistas of glorious scenery. Wildlife in the Cairngorms is unequalled elsewhere in Britain, and here it is brought to the binoculars of any walker who treads quietly and with respect.

# NATURAL SCOTLAND

## Wild Scotland: The essential guide to finding the best of natural Scotland

James McCarthy

Photography by Laurie Campbell

ISBN 0 946487 37 5  PBK £7.50

With a foreword by Magnus Magnusson and striking colour photographs by Laurie Campbell, this is the essential up-to-date guide to viewing wildlife in Scotland for the visitor and resident alike. It provides a fascinating overview of the country's plants, animals, bird and marine life against the background of their typical natural settings, as an introduction to the vivid descriptions of the most accessible localities, linked to clear regional maps. A unique feature is the focus on 'green tourism' and sustainable visitor use of the countryside, contributed by Duncan Bryden, manager of the Scottish Tourist Board's Tourism and the Environment Task Force. Important practical information on access and the best times of year for viewing sites makes this an indispensable and user-friendly travelling companion to anyone interested in exploring Scotland's remarkable natural heritage.

James McCarthy is former Deputy Director for Scotland of the Nature Conservancy Council, and now a Board Member of Scottish Natural Heritage and Chairman of the Environmental Youth Work National Development Project Scotland.

## 'Nothing but Heather!'

Gerry Cambridge

ISBN 0 946487 49 9 PBK £15.00

Enter the world of Scottish nature – bizarre, brutal, often beautiful, always fascinating – as seen through the lens and poems of Gerry Cam-bridge, one of Scotland's most distinctive contemporary poets.

On film and in words, Cambridge brings unusual focus to bear on lives as diverse as those of dragonflies, hermit crabs, short-eared owls, and wood anemones. The result is both an instructive look by a naturalist at some of the flora and fauna of Scotland and a poet's aesthetic journey. This exceptional collection comprises 48 poems matched with 48 captioned photographs. In his introduction Cambridge explores the origins of the project and the approaches to nature taken by other poets, and incorporates a wry account of an unwillingly-sectarian, farm-labouring, bird-obsessed adolescence in rural Ayrshire in the 1970s.

*Keats felt that the beauty of a rainbow was somehow tarnished by knowledge of its properties. Yet the natural world is surely made more, not less, marvellous by awareness of its workings. In the poems that accompany these pictures, I have tried to give an inkling of that. May the marriage of verse and image enlarge the reader's appreciation and, perhaps, insight into the chomping, scurrying, quivering, procreating and dying kingdom, however many miles it be beyond the door.* GERRY CAMBRIDGE

*'a real poet, with a sense of the music of language and the poetry of life...'* KATHLEEN RAINE

*'one of the most promising and original of modern Scottish poets... a master of form and subtlety.'* GEORGE MACKAY BROWN

## Scotland Land and People
## An Inhabited Solitude

James McCarthy

ISBN 0 946487 57 X PBK £7.99

*'Scotland is the country above all others that I have seen, in which a man of imagination may carve out his own pleasures; there are so many inhabited solitudes.'*
DOROTH WORDSWORTH, in her journal of August 1803

An informed and thought-provoking profile of Scotland's unique landscapes and the impact of humans on what we see now and in the future. James McCarthy leads us through the many aspects of the land and the people who inhabit it: natural Scotland; the rocks beneath; land ownership; the use of resources; people and place; conserving Scotland's heritage and much more.

Written in a highly readable style, this concise volume offers an under-standing of the land as a whole. Emphasising the uniqueness of the Scottish environment, the author explores the links between this and other aspects of our culture as a key element in rediscovering a modern sense of the Scottish identity and perception of nationhood.

*'This book provides an engaging introduction to the mysteries of Scotland's people and landscapes. Difficult concepts are described in simple terms, providing the interested Scot or tourist with an invaluable overview of the country... It fills an important niche which, to my knowledge, is filled by no other publications.'*
BETSY KING, Chief Executive, Scottish Environmental Education Council.

## The Highland Geology Trail

John L Roberts

ISBN 0946487 36 7 PBK £4.99

Where can you find the oldest rocks in Europe?

Where can you see ancient hills around 800 million years old?

How do you tell whether a valley was carved out by a glacier, not a river?

What are the Fucoid Beds?

Where do you find rocks folded like putty?

How did great masses of rock pile up like snow in front of a snow-plough?

When did volcanoes spew lava and ash to form Skye, Mull and Rum?

Where can you find fossils on Skye?

*'...a lucid introduction to the geological record in general, a jargon-free exposition of the regional*

background, and a series of descriptions of specific localities of geological interest on a "trail" around the highlands.

Having checked out the local references on the ground, I can vouch for their accuracy and look forward to investigating farther afield, informed by this guide.

Great care has been taken to explain specific terms as they occur and, in so doing, John Roberts has created a resource of great value which is eminently usable by anyone with an interest in the outdoors...the best bargain you are likely to get as a geology book in the foreseeable future.'
Jim Johnston, PRESS AND JOURNAL

## Rum: Nature's Island

Magnus Magnusson

ISBN 0 946487 32 4   £7.95 PBK

*Rum: Nature's Island* is the fascinating story of a Hebridean island from the earliest times through to the Clearances and its period as the sporting playground of a Lancashire industrial magnate, and on to its rebirth as a National Nature Reserve, a model for the active ecological management of Scotland's wild places.

Thoroughly researched and written in a lively accessible style, the book includes comprehensive coverage of the island's geology, animals and plants, and people, with a special chapter on the Edwardian extravaganza of Kinloch Castle. There is practical information for visitors to what was once known as 'the Forbidden Isle'; the book provides details of bothy and other accommodation, walks and nature trails. It closes with a positive vision for the island's future: biologically diverse, economically dynamic and ecologically sustainable.

*Rum: Nature's Island* is published in co-operation with Scottish Natural Heritage (of which Magnus Magnusson is Chairman) to mark the 40th anniversary of the acquisition of Rum by its predecessor, The Nature Conservancy.

# ON THE TRAIL OF

## On the Trail of William Wallace

David R. Ross

ISBN 0 946487 47 2   PBK   £7.99

How close to reality was *Braveheart*?

Where was Wallace actually born?

What was the relationship between Wallace and Bruce?

Are there any surviving eye-witness accounts of Wallace?

How does Wallace influence the psyche of today's Scots?

*On the Trail of William Wallace* offers a refreshing insight into the life and heritage of the great Scots hero whose proud story is at the very heart of what it means to be Scottish.

Not concentrating simply on the hard historical facts of Wallace's life, the book also takes into account the real significance of Wallace and his effect on the ordinary Scot through the ages, manifested in the many sites where his memory is marked.

In trying to piece together the jigsaw of the reality of Wallace's life, David Ross weaves a subtle flow of new information with his own observations. His engaging, thoughtful and at times amusing narrative reads with the ease of a historical novel, complete with all the intrigue, treachery and romance required to hold the attention of the casual reader and still entice the more knowledgable historian.

74 places to visit in Scotland and the north of England

One general map and 3 location maps

Stirling and Falkirk battle plans

Wallace's route through London

Chapter on Wallace connections in North America and elsewhere

Reproductions of rarely seen illustrations

*On the Trail of William Wallace* will be enjoyed by anyone with an interest in Scotland, from the passing tourist to the most fervent nationalist. It is an encyclopaedia-cum-guide book, literally stuffed with fascinating titbits not usually on offer in the conventional history book.

David Ross is organiser of and historical adviser to the Society of William Wallace.

'*Historians seem to think all there is to be known about Wallace has already been uncovered. Mr Ross has proved that Wallace studies are in fact in their infancy.*' ELSPETH KING, Director of the Stirling Smith Art Museum & Gallery, who annotated and introduced the recent Luath edition of *Blind Harry's Wallace.*

'*Better the pen than the sword!*' RANDALL WALLACE, author of *Braveheart*, when asked by David Ross how it felt to be partly responsible for the freedom of a nation following the Devolution Referendum.

## On the Trail of Robert the Bruce

David R. Ross

ISBN 0 946487 52 9   PBK   £7.99

*On the Trail of Robert the Bruce* charts the story of Scotland's hero-king from his boyhood, through his days of indecision as Scotland suffered under the English yoke, to his assumption of the crown exactly six months after the death of William Wallace. Here is the astonishing blow by blow account of how, against fearful odds, Bruce led the Scots to win their greatest ever victory Bannockburn was not the end of the story. The war against English oppression lasted another fourteen years. Bruce lived just long enough to see his dreams of an independent Scotland come to fruition in 1328 with the signing of the Treaty of Edinburgh. The trail takes us to Bruce sites in Scotland, many of the little known and forgotten battle sites in northern England, and as far afield as the Bruce monuments in Andalusia and Jerusalem.

67 places to visit in Scotland and elsewhere.

One general map, 3 location maps and a map of Bruce-connected sites in Ireland.

Bannockburn battle plan.

Drawings and reproductions of rarely seen illustrations.

*On the Trail of Robert the Bruce* is not all blood and gore. It brings out the love and laughter, pain and passion of one of the great eras of Scottish history. Read it and you will understand why David Ross has never knowingly killed a spider in his life. Once again, he proves himself a master of the popular brand of hands-on history that made *On the Trail of William Wallace* so popular.

'*David R. Ross is a proud patriot and unashamed romantic.*'

SCOTLAND ON SUNDAY

'*Robert the Bruce knew Scotland, knew every class of her people, as no man who ruled her before or since has done. It was he who asked of her a miracle - and she accomplished it.*' AGNES MUIR MACKENZIE

## On the Trail of Robert Service

GW Lockhart

ISBN 0 946487 24 3 PBK £7.99

Robert Service is famed world-wide for his eye-witness verse-pictures of the Klondike goldrush. As a war poet, his work outsold Owen and Sassoon, and he went on to become the world's first million selling poet. In search of adventure and new experiences, he emigrated from Scotland to Canada in 1890 where he was caught up in the aftermath of

the raging gold fever. His vivid dramatic verse bring to life the wild, larger than life characters of the gold rush Yukon, their bar-room brawls, their lust for gold, their trigger-happy gambles with life and love. 'The Shooting of Dan McGrew' is perhaps his most famous poem:

*A bunch of the boys were whooping it up in the Malamute saloon;*
*The kid that handles the music box was hitting a ragtime tune;*
*Back of the bar in a solo game, sat Dangerous Dan McGrew,*
*And watching his luck was his light o'love, the lady that's known as Lou.*

His storytelling powers have brought Robert Service enduring fame, particularly in North America and Scotland where he is something of a cult figure.

Starting in Scotland, *On the Trail of Robert Service* follows Service as he wanders through British Columbia, Oregon, California, Mexico, Cuba, Tahiti, Russia, Turkey and the Balkans, finally 'settling' in France.

'*A fitting tribute to a remarkable man - a bank clerk who wanted to become a cowboy. It is hard to imagine a bank clerk writing such lines as:*
*A bunch of boys were whooping it up...*
*The income from his writing actually exceeded his bank salary by a factor of five and he resigned to pursue a full time writing career.*' Charles Munn, THE SCOTTISH BANKER

'*Robert Service claimed he wrote for those who wouldn't be seen dead reading poetry. His was an almost unbelievably mobile life... Lockhart hangs on breathlessly, enthusiastically unearthing clues to the poet's life.*' Ruth Thomas, SCOTTISH BOOK COLLECTOR

'*This enthralling biography will delight Service lovers in both the Old World and the New.*' Marilyn Wright, SCOTS INDEPENDENT

## On the Trail of Mary Queen of Scots

J. Keith Cheetham

ISBN 0 946487 50 2 PBK £7.99

Life dealt Mary Queen of Scots love, intrigue, betrayal and tragedy in generous measure.

*On the Trail of Mary Queen of Scots* traces the major events in the turbulent life of the beautiful, enigmatic queen whose romantic reign and tragic destiny exerts an undimmed fascination over 400 years after her execution.

Places of interest to visit - 99 in Scotland, 35 in England and 29 in France.

One general map and 6 location maps.

Line drawings and illustrations.
Simplified family tree of the royal houses of Tudor and Stuart.

Key sites include:

Linlithgow Palace - Mary's birthplace, now a magnificent ruin

Stirling Castle – where, only nine months old, Mary was crowned Queen of Scotland

Notre Dame Cathedral – where, aged fifteen, she married the future king of France

The Palace of Holyroodhouse – Rizzio, one of Mary's closest advisers, was murdered here and some say his blood still stains the spot where he was stabbed to death

Sheffield Castle – where for fourteen years she languished as prisoner of her cousin, Queen Elizabeth I

Fotheringhay – here Mary finally met her death on the executioner's block.

*On the Trail of Mary Queen of Scots* is for everyone interested in the life of perhaps the most romantic figure in Scotland's history; a thorough guide to places connected with Mary, it is also a guide to the complexities of her personal and public life.

*'In my end is my beginning'* MARY QUEEN OF SCOTS

*'...the woman behaves like the Whore of Babylon'* JOHN KNOX

# MUSIC AND DANCE

## Highland Balls and Village Halls

GW Lockhart

ISBN 0 946487 12 X  PBK  £6.95

Acknowledged as a classic in Scottish dancing circles throughout the world. Anecdotes, Scottish history, dress and dance steps are all included in this *'delightful little book, full of interest... both a personal account and an understanding look at the making of traditions.'*
NEW ZEALAND SCOTTISH COUNTRY DANCES MAGAZINE

*'A delightful survey of Scottish dancing and custom. Informative, concise and opinionated, it guides the reader across the history and geography of country dance and ends by detailing the 12 dances every Scot should know – the most famous being the Eightsome Reel, "the greatest longest, rowdiest, most diabolically executed of all the Scottish country dances".'* THE HERALD

*'A pot-pourri of every facet of Scottish country dancing. It will bring back memories of petronella turns and poussettes and make you eager to take part in a Broun's reel or a dashing white sergeant!'*

DUNDEE COURIER AND ADVERTISER
*'An excellent an very readable insight into the traditions and customs of Scottish country dancing. The author takes us on a tour from his own early days jigging in the village hall to the characters and traditions that have made our own brand of dance popular throughout the world.'* SUNDAY POST

## Fiddles & Folk: A celebration of the re-emergence of Scotland's musical heritage

GW Lockhart

ISBN 0 946487 38 3  PBK  £7.95

In *Fiddles & Folk*, his companion volume to *Highland Balls and Village Halls*, Wallace Lockhart meets up with many of the people who have created the renaissance of Scotland's music at home and overseas.

From Dougie MacLean, Hamish Henderson, the Battlefield Band, the Whistlebinkies, the Scottish Fiddle Orchestra, the McCalmans and many more come the stories that break down the musical barriers between Scotland's past and present, and between the diverse musical forms which have woven together to create the dynamism of the music today.

*'I have tried to avoid a formal approach to Scottish music as it affects those of us with our musical heritage coursing through our veins. The picture I have sought is one of many brush strokes, looking at how some individuals have come to the fore, examining their music, lives, thoughts, even philosophies...'*
WALLACE LOCKHART

*' "I never had a narrow, woolly-jumper, fingers stuck in the ear approach to music. We have a musical heritage here that is the envy of the rest of the world. Most countries just can't compete," he [Ian Green, Greentrax] says. And as young Scots tire of Oasis and Blur, they will realise that there is a wealth of young Scottish music on their doorstep just waiting to be discovered.'* THE SCOTSMAN

For anyone whose heart lifts at the sound of fiddle or pipes, this book takes you on a delightful journey, full of humour and respect, in the company of some of the performers who have taken Scotland's music around the world and come back enriched.

# NEW SCOTLAND

## Old Scotland New Scotland

Jeff Fallow

ISBN 0 946487 40 5 PBK £6.99

'Together we can build a new Scotland based on Labour's values.' DONALD DEWAR, Party Political Broadcast

'Despite the efforts of decent Mr Dewar, the voters may yet conclude they are looking at the same old hacks in brand new suits.' IAN BELL, *The Independent*

'At times like this you suddenly realise how dangerous the neglect of Scottish history in our schools and universities may turn out to be.' MICHAEL FRY, *The Herald*

'...one of the things I hope will go is our chip on the shoulder about the English... The SNP has a huge responsibility to articulate Scottish independence in a way that is pro-Scottish and not anti-English.' ALEX SALMOND, *The Scotsman*

Scottish politics have never been more exciting. In *old Scotland new Scotland* Jeff Fallow takes us on a graphic voyage through Scotland's turbulent history, from earliest times through to the present day and beyond. This fast-track guide is the quick way to learn what your history teacher didn't tell you, essential reading for all who seek an understanding of Scotland and its history.

Eschewing the romanticisation of his country's past, Fallow offers a new perspective on an old nation. 'Too many people associate Scottish history with tartan trivia or outworn romantic myth. This book aims to blast that stubborn idea.' JEFF FALLOW

## Scotland - Land and Power
## the agenda for land reform

Andy Wightman
in association with
Democratic Left Scotland
foreword by Lesley Riddoch

ISBN 0 946487 70 7 PBK £5.00

What is land reform?
Why is it needed?
Will the Scottish Parliament really make a difference? *Scotland – Land and Power* argues passionately that nothing less than a radical, comprehensive programme of land reform can make the difference that is needed. Now is no time for palliative solutions which treat the symptoms and not the causes.

*Scotland – Land and Power* is a controversial and provocative book that clarifies the complexities of landownership in Scotland. Andy Wightman explodes the myth that land issues are relevant only to the far flung fringes of rural Scotland, and questions mainstream political commitment to land reform. He presents his own far-reaching programme for change and a pragmatic, inspiring vision of how Scotland can move from outmoded, unjust power structures towards a more equitable landowning democracy.

'Writers like Andy Wightman are determined to make sure that the hurt of the last century is not compounded by a rushed solution in the next. This accessible, comprehensive but passionately argued book is quite simply essential reading and perfectly timed – here's hoping Scotland's legislators agree.'
LESLEY RIDDOCH

## Notes from the North
## incorporating a Brief History of the Scots and the English

Emma Wood

ISBN 0 946487 46 4 PBK £8.99

Notes on being English
Notes on being in Scotland
Learning from a shared past

Sickened by the English jingoism that surfaced in rampant form during the 1982 Falklands War, Emma Wood started to dream of moving from her home in East Anglia to the Highlands of Scotland. She felt increasingly frustrated and marginalised as Thatcherism got a grip on the southern English psyche. The Scots she met on frequent holidays in the Highlands had no truck with Thatcherism, and she felt at home with grass-roots Scottish anti-authoritarianism. The decision was made. She uprooted and headed for a new life in the north of Scotland.

'*An intelligent and perceptive book... calm, reflective, witty and sensitive. It should certainly be read by all English visitors to Scotland, be they tourists or incomers. And it should certainly be read by all Scots concerned about what kind of nation we live in. They might learn something about themselves.*'
THE HERALD

'*... her enlightenment is evident on every page of this perceptive, provocative book.*'
MAIL ON SUNDAY

# BIOGRAPHY

## Tobermory Teuchter: A first-hand account of life on Mull in the early years of the 20th century

Peter Macnab

ISBN 0 946487 41 3  PBK  £7.99

Peter Macnab was reared on Mull, as was his father, and his grandfather before him. In this book he provides a revealing account of life on Mull during the first quarter of the 20th century, focusing especially on the years of World War I. This enthralling social history of the island is set against Peter Macnab's early years as son of the governor of the Mull Poorhouse, one of the last in the Hebrides, and is illustrated throughout by photo-graphs from his exceptional collection. Peter Macnab's 'fisherman's yarns' and other personal reminis-cences are told delightfully by a born storyteller.

This latest work from the author of a range of books about the island, including the standard study of Mull and Iona, reveals his unparallelled knowledge of and deep feeling for Mull and its people. After his long career with the Clydesdale Bank, first in Tobermory and later on the mainland, Peter, now 94, remains a teuchter at heart, proud of his island heritage.

'Peter Macnab is a man of words who doesnit mince his words - not where his beloved Mull is concerned. 'I will never forget some of the inmates of the poorhouse,' says Peter. 'Some of them were actually victims of the later Clearances. It was history at first hand, and there was no romance about it'. But Peter Macnab sees little creative point in crying over ancient injustices. For him the task is to help Mull in this century and beyond.'
SCOTS MAGAZINE, May 1998

## Bare Feet and Tackety Boots

Archie Cameron

ISBN 0 946487 17 0  PBK  £7.95

The island of Rum before the First World War was the playground of its rich absentee landowner. A survivor of life a century gone tells his story. Factors and schoolmasters, midges and poaching, deer, ducks and MacBrayne's steamers: here social history and personal anecdote create a record of a way of life gone not long ago but already almost forgotten. This is the story the gentry couldn't tell.

'This book is an important piece of social history, for it gives an insight into how the other half lived

in an era the likes of which will never be seen again' FORTHRIGHT MAGAZINE
'The authentic breath of the pawky, country-wise estate employee.' THE OBSERVER
'Well observed and detailed account of island life in the early years of this century'. THE SCOTS MAGAZINE
'A very good read with the capacity to make the reader chuckle. A very talented writer.' STORNOWAY GAZETTE

## Come Dungeons Dark

John Taylor Caldwell

ISBN 0 946487 19 7  PBK  £6.95

Glasgow anarchist Guy Aldred died with 10p in his pocket in 1963 claiming there was better company in Barlinnie Prison than in the Corridors of Power. 'The Red Scourge' is remembered here by one who worked with him and spent 27 years as part of his turbulent household, sparring with Lenin, Sylvia Pankhurst and others as he struggled for freedom for his beloved fellow-man.

'The welcome and long-awaited biography of... one of this country's most prolific radical propagandists... Crank or visionary?... whatever the verdict, the Glasgow anarchist has finally been given a fitting memorial.' THE SCOTSMAN

# FICTION

## Grave Robbers

Robin Mitchell

ISBN 0 946487 72 3

After years of sleeping peacefully, the deceased dignitaries of Old Edinburgh are about to get a nasty surprise.......

Grave-digger and funeral enthusiast Cameron Carter lives a relatively quiet life. Until a misplaced shovel cracks open a coffin lid and reveals a hidden fortune, that is. Nearly one hundred and seventy years after the trial of Scotland's notorious body snatchers, William Burke and William Hare, the ancient trade of grave robbing returns to the town's cemeteries.

Forming an unholy union with small time crook, Adam, Cameron is drawn into a web of crime that involves a bogus American Scholars' Society, chocolate chip ice cream and Steve McQueen. Their sacrilegious scheming doesn't go quite to plan, however, and events begin to spiral dangerously beyond Cameron the answers will be exhumed.

Will our hero pull the tour guide of his dreams?

Will his partner in crime ever shift those microwaves?

Is there an afterlife?

In Robin Mitchell's rude and darkly comic debut novel, all the answers will be exhumed.

*'Good, unclean macabre fun from Robin Mitchell...'*
IAN RANKIN

### The Bannockburn Years
William Scott
ISBN 0 946487 34 0  PBK  £7.95

 A present day Edinburgh solicitor stumbles across reference to a document of value to the Nation State of Scotland. He tracks down the document on the Isle of Bute, a document which probes the real 'quaestiones' about nationhood and national identity. The document ends up being published, but is it authentic and does it matter? Almost 700 years on, these 'quaestiones' are still worth asking.

Written with pace and passion, William Scott has devised an intriguing vehicle to open up new ways of looking at the future of Scotland and its people. He presents an alternative interpretation of how the Battle of Bannockburn was fought, and through the Bannatyne manuscript he draws the reader into the minds of those involved.

Winner of the 1997 Constable Trophy, the premier award in Scotland for an unpublished novel, this book offers new insights to both the academic and the general reader which are sure to provoke further discussion and debate.

*'A brilliant storyteller. I shall expect to see your name writ large hereafter.'*
NIGEL TRANTER, October 1997.

*'... a compulsive read.'* PH Scott, THE SCOTSMAN

### The Great Melnikov
Hugh MacLachlan
ISBN 0 946487 42 1  PBK £7.95

A well crafted, gripping novel, written in a style reminiscent of John Buchan and set in London and the Scottish Highlands during the First World War, *The Great Melnikov* is a dark tale of double-cross and deception. We first meet Melnikov, one-time star of the German circus, languishing as a down-and-out in Trafalgar

 Square. He soon finds himself drawn into a tortuous web of intrigue. He is a complex man whose personal struggle with alcoholism is an inner drama which parallels the tense twists and turns as a spy mystery unfolds. Melnikov's options are narrowing. The circle of threat is closing. Will Melnikov outwit the sinister enemy spy network? Can he summon the will and the wit to survive?

Hugh MacLachlan, in his first full length novel, demonstrates an undoubted ability to tell a good story well. His earlier stories have been broadcast on Radio Scotland, and he has the rare distinction of being shortlisted for the Macallan/Scotland on Sunday Short Story Competition two years in succession.

## SPORT

### Over the Top with the Tartan Army (Active Service 1992-97)
Andrew McArthur
ISBN 0 946487 45 6  PBK  £7.99

 Scotland has witnessed the growth of a new and curious military phenomenon – grown men bedecked in tartan yom-ping across the globe, hell-bent on benevolence and ritualistic bevvying. What noble cause does this famous army serve? Why, football of course!

Taking us on an erratic world tour, McArthur gives a frighteningly funny insider's eye view of active service with the Tartan Army – the madcap antics of Scotland's travelling support in the '90s, written from the inside, covering campaigns and skirmishes from Euro '92 up to the qualifying drama for France '98 in places as diverse as Russia, the Faroes, Belarus, Sweden, Monte Carlo, Estonia, Latvia, USA and Finland.

This book is a must for any football fan who likes a good laugh.

*'I commend this book to all football supporters'.* Graham Spiers, SCOTLAND ON SUNDAY

*'In wishing Andy McArthur all the best with this publication, I do hope he will be in a position to produce a sequel after our participation in the World Cup in France'.* CRAIG BROWN, Scotland Team Coach

All royalties on sales of the book are going to Scottish charities.

### Ski & Snowboard Scotland

Hilary Parke

ISBN 0 946487 35 9 PBK £6.99

Snowsports in Scotland are still a secret treasure. There's no need to go abroad when there's such an exciting variety of terrain right here on your doorstep. You just need to know what to look for. *Ski & Snowboard Scotland* is aimed at maximising the time you have available so that the hours you spend on the snow are memorable for all the right reasons.

This fun and informative book guides you over the slopes of Scotland, giving you the inside track on all the major ski centres. There are chapters ranging from how to get there to the impact of snowsports on the environment.

'*Reading the book brought back many happy memories of my early training days at the dry slope in Edinburgh and of many brilliant weekends in the Cairngorms.*'

EMMA CARRICK-ANDERSON, from her foreword, written in the US, during a break in training for her first World Cup as a member of the British Alpine Ski Team.

# SOCIAL HISTORY

## A Word for Scotland

Jack Campbell

with a foreword by Magnus Magnusson

ISBN 0 946487 48 0 PBK £12.99

'A word for Scotland' was Lord Beaverbrook's hope when he founded the *Scottish Daily Express*. That word for Scotland quickly became, and was for many years, the national newspaper of Scotland.

The pages of *A Word For Scotland* exude warmth and a wry sense of humour. Jack Campbell takes us behind the scenes to meet the larger-than-life characters and ordinary people who made and recorded the stories. Here we hear the stories behind the stories that hit the headlines in this great yarn of journalism in action.

It would be true to say 'all life is here'. From the Cheapside Street fire of which cost the lives of 19 Glasgow firemen, to the theft of the Stone of Destiny, to the lurid exploits of serial killer Peter Manuel, to encounters with world boxing champions Benny Lynch and Cassius Clay - this book offers telling glimpses of the characters, events, joy and tragedy which make up Scotland's story in the 20th century.

'*As a rookie reporter you were proud to work on it and proud to be part of it - it was fine newspaper right at the heartbeat of Scotland.*'

RONALD NEIL, Chief Executive of BBC Production, and a reporter on the *Scottish Daily Express* (1963-68)

'*This book is a fascinating reminder of Scottish journalism in its heyday. It will be read avidly by those journalists who take pride in their profession – and should be compulsory reading for those who don't.*'

JACK WEBSTER, columnist on *The Herald* and *Scottish Daily Express* journalist (1960-80)

## The Crofting Years

Francis Thompson

ISBN 0 946487 06 5 PBK £6.95

Crofting is much more than a way of life. It is a storehouse of cultural, linguistic and moral values which holds together a scattered and struggling rural population. This book fills a blank in the written history of crofting over the last two centuries.

Bloody conflicts and gunboat diplomacy, treachery, compassion, music and story: all figure in this mine of information on crofting in the Highlands and Islands of Scotland.

'*I would recommend this book to all who are interested in the past, but even more so to those who are interested in the future survival of our way of life and culture*' STORNOWAY GAZETTE

'*The book is a mine of information on many aspects of the past, among them the homes, the food, the music and the medicine of our crofting forebears.*'

John M Macmillan, erstwhile CROFTERS COMMISSIONER FOR LEWIS AND HARRIS

# POETRY

## Blind Harry's Wallace

William Hamilton of Gilbertfield

Introduced by Elspeth King

ISBN 0 946487 43 X HBK £15.00

ISBN 0 946487 33 2 PBK £8.99

The original story of the real braveheart, Sir William Wallace. Racy, blood on every page, violently anglo-phobic, grossly embellished, vulgar and disgus-ting, clumsy and stilted, a literary failure, a great epic.

Whatever the verdict on BLIND HARRY, this is the